I'M WORKING ON IT IN THERAPY

How to Get the Most out of Psychotherapy

GARY TROSCLAIR

Skyhorse Publishing

Skyhorse Publishing books may be purchased in bulk at special discounts for sales promotion, corporate gifts, fund-raising, or educational purposes. Special editions can also be created to specifications. For details, contact the Special Sales Department, Skyhorse Publishing, 307 West 36th Street, 11th Floor, New York, NY 10018 or info@skyhorsepublishing.com.

Skyhorse® and Skyhorse Publishing® are registered trademarks of Skyhorse Publishing, Inc.®, a Delaware corporation.

Visit our website at www.skyhorsepublishing.com.

10 9 8 7 6 5 4 3 2 1

Library of Congress Cataloging-in-Publication Data is available on file.

Cover design by Eric Kang

Print ISBN: 978-1-63220-448-6
Ebook ISBN: 978-1-63220-748-7
Printed in the United States of America

Cartoons used by permission, as follows:
Alex Gregory /The New Yorker Collection/www.cartoonbank.com
Charles Barsotti /The New Yorker Collection/www.cartoonbank.com
Danny Shanahan /The New Yorker Collection/www.cartoonbank.com
David Sipress /The New Yorker Collection/www.cartoonbank.com
David Stein /The New Yorker Collection/www.cartoonbank.com
J.B. Handelsman /The New Yorker Collection/www.cartoonbank.com
Michael Crawford /The New Yorker Collection/www.cartoonbank.com
Mick Stevens /The New Yorker Collection/www.cartoonbank.com
Mike Twohy /The New Yorker Collection/www.cartoonbank.com
Leo Cullum /The New Yorker Collection/www.cartoonbank.com
Robert Mankoff /The New Yorker Collection/www.cartoonbank.com

Contents

Dedication

For all those who have worked with me, in
appreciation for your trust, and your commitment
to an endeavor that benefits us all.

Preface

"So what am I supposed to *DO?* What do I have to do to change?" It was shortly after I'd finished my postgraduate training when Edward, a sturdy young account manager sitting across from me in my office, asked these questions. He'd come to therapy to address his reactive anger and what he recognized as an otherwise shut-down emotional life. "I told my friends I'm working on it in therapy, but to be honest, I have no bloody idea what that really means." This was his third month in therapy and we were beginning to gain insight into some of his issues. He was eager to make progress and was willing to work, but he was at a loss as to what he needed to do to make therapy effective.

I had to sit back and reflect. It seemed like it should be an easy question, one that I should be able to answer immediately. But the training and study I had done hadn't focused on what the client needed to do; we had focused only on our role as therapists.

Thinking on the fly, I told him that his job was to bring himself—each and every part of himself—into our meetings as completely as possible, to tell me about every little scrap of joy or frustration or vulnerability or any other feeling that flashed across his screen before it got deleted by his censors. But I also wanted him to contain these feelings—not to react to them—so that we could get to know them first. I told him that he was already doing that by being direct with me about his frustration. I also suggested that we both get very curious—without judgment—about the patterns and the stories that went along with these emotions, not to get lost in the details, but to try to keep the big picture in mind so that we could challenge those stories when we needed to. I told him that there would be more he could do, but that would make for a good start.

Since then many clients have asked me what they need to do to make the process successful, and many have asked me to recommend a book to help them understand the process. I appreciate their willingness to take an active role in the work, and I try to give them some guidelines about how to make the best use of their experience in therapy. But I've found that anything other than the briefest instructions in session can be onerous and disruptive, and I've never found a book that I felt I could recommend to explain what they needed to do to make the process effective. Plenty of books tell the therapist what to do, and many other books give hints about what clients might need to talk about in therapy to deal with their specific issue. But clients are generally left with little guidance and many questions about how to actually proceed:

- What are people doing in their sessions when things are going well?
- How do I know if I'm making the best use of my investment there?
- Is there anything that I need to do, or is it the therapist's insight and empathy that will change me?
- Should I vent or be objective and analytical?
- Is there anything I'm supposed to do outside of the session?

When I first considered writing a book that would answer these questions, I had my misgivings. Therapy is ideally an organic process; it flows spontaneously and whatever arises in sessions serves as the basis for the work. I didn't want to disrupt that spontaneous flow with instructions. But the more I thought about it, the more it seemed to me that a guide to psychotherapy could actually help clients to see the value of first being spontaneous and then reflecting on whatever came up, and that I could encourage them to dive in and use both.

So what *does* it mean to "work on it" in psychotherapy? This book is an answer to these questions and similar ones that I've heard from clients in the years since Edward first prompted my interest in the subject. I've written *I'm Working on It in Therapy: How to Get the Most Out of Psychotherapy* to demystify the client's role in psychotherapy so that those of you who are in therapy can make the most of your experience. I've also written it so that those of you who are considering entering psychotherapy can get a more realistic sense of what it entails. I offer it too as a resource for other therapists, that it might enrich your work, and that it might stimulate more thinking and discussion about how we can help our clients get the most out of psychotherapy.

This book will convey the client's role in therapy as I've come to understand it through twenty-five years of practicing therapy and teaching the process to advanced students. I will share stories of what clients have done to make their experience in therapy successful, and stories from literature and mythology that demonstrate what heroes and heroines have done for millennia to achieve change. I will also draw upon recent research that helps us to understand how to use psychotherapy effectively.

I hope that this book will help you to use your therapist as a guide and partner in your own process of discovery. I believe that the human psyche has an innate aspiration to heal and grow, a constructive unconscious (which I'll describe in Chapter Three). If you and your therapist are both enlisting this natural tendency, the energy that arises will be very productive. I also believe that taking an active role in improving our lives helps us to develop a powerful sense of mastery and agency that is in itself healing.

This book describes ten tools that you can use to "work on it." Once you've finished reading it, you will have a very good sense of what you need to do in therapy to use it effectively. If at any point in your work you feel lost or stuck, I'd suggest that you review the chapter headings and the summaries at the end of each chapter to see if there is a particular tool that you could exercise more to get things moving again.

When heroes and heroines set off on adventures of self-discovery, they're usually given something to help them pass the trials they encounter so they can get to where they need to go: an ancient and revered weapon, a magic flute, a tiny wooden doll, a special coin to pay for the ferry across a river, a piece of wisdom, or any of a thousand other articles that symbolize methods for handling ordeals. No one can tell them exactly where they need to go or what problems they will run into, but the "tools" they receive are indispensable for them to navigate the challenges ahead of them. My hope is that these tools will serve you on your heroic journey into your own uncharted territory.

Introduction and a Few Things to Know Before Reading This Book

The *content* of therapy—the specifics of what therapists and clients talk about in sessions—varies widely from person to person, and can't be prescribed. But the *process* of therapy—the how—includes essential practices that are crucial to know, whether it's depression, anxiety, relationship issues, addictions, general well-being, or any other issues that bring you into therapy. These tools, as I'll call them, constitute the heart and soul of "working on it" in therapy. Learning to use these tools consciously helps clients who have engaged in psychotherapy continue to benefit from the process long after they've stopped seeing their therapist.

These tools are no secret, yet they are not well known. And because they are so rarely discussed, distorted portrayals of psychotherapy have filled the vacuum.

If you were to base your idea of what you need to do in therapy on conventional conceptions, some of them found in the media, you might wait a long time for your therapist to say something insightful that would suddenly change you. Television and film generally use dramatic moments to entertain us, and the real, more incremental, work that the client does in therapy isn't always portrayed.

Older, stereotypical conceptions of therapy portray a removed and reserved analyst sitting out of sight behind a couch making observations that enlighten you. More recent conceptions may evoke a nurturing and empathic, but not-so-challenging, therapist who sits across from you and supports you until your wounds are healed.

Either version may leave you in a passive state, believing that your therapist's insights or nurturing will be sufficient to bring about the change you want. Misconceptions about how therapy works may keep some people from entering therapy and reaping its benefits, keep others from sticking with therapy long enough to get help they need, and keep others attending sessions long past the point of diminishing returns.

An increasing body of evidence suggests that it's not what the therapist does, or even a particular model of therapy, that accounts for change; rather it's the client's involvement, participation, and contribution that actually accounts for most of the progress in therapy.[1]

Psychotherapy works less like going to a guru for answers, and more like engaging in a personal and collaborative exploration, one that asks you to bring out, test, and develop your own ideas, feelings, and behavior in the sessions themselves. It's less like massage and more like physical therapy, which requires a fair amount of stretching and effort on your part.

The reality is that it's difficult to achieve significant personal change and that it does take work. If, as therapists, we let you believe otherwise, we're misleading you, and any therapist that does mislead you that way should be tarred and feathered. Therapy is a heroic venture that requires both initiative and receptivity, neither of which is easy. The very nature of the work requires us to go to the places that scare us most, and it can feel incredibly difficult at times to remain open and persevere.

But the good news is that psychotherapy does make change possible. There is accumulating research evidence (see Appendix C) that demonstrates the enduring efficacy of psychotherapy. We now know that therapy literally changes the neurological wiring in our brains.[2]

Understanding your role in accomplishing that change is key to gaining the maximum benefits of the process and in maintaining those benefits once you've stopped attending sessions.

TEN TOOLS

I've organized the work of therapy into ten tools, ten overlapping ways to use the process effectively, and described each of them in a separate chapter. I've tried to lay these out in an order that bears some resemblance to when you might experience them in your process, but they really aren't so distinct, and you don't need to exercise them in a particular sequence in your actual work. However, it will be most helpful to read the chapters in order, because my explanations do build on each other.

Following are the ten tools. But before you read them, I'd suggest you take a few minutes to list the things that you believe you need to do to make psychotherapy work for you. This could come in handy later in discussions with your therapist.

1. *Get real:* Take off the mask and show your many faces.
2. *Channel the flow of feeling:* Have your feelings without your feelings having you.
3. *Enough about them:* Look deeply within for the sources of change.
4. *Don't hold back:* Forge an authentic connection with your therapist.
5. *Be curious, not judgmental:* Observe yourself honestly without attacking yourself.
6. *Carry only your fair share:* Differentiate when to take responsibility and when not to.
7. *What's your story?* Identify the recurring themes and fundamental beliefs that guide your life.
8. *It ain't necessarily so:* Build a better narrative and choose your beliefs consciously.
9. *Do something!* Continue your psychological work outside of sessions.
10. *Into the fire:* Use the challenges of your life as opportunities for growth.

A FEW THINGS TO KNOW BEFORE READING THIS BOOK

I've included condensed case examples of typical situations in order to give you a clearer idea of how these tools work. In order to protect my clients' privacy, these examples are composites that don't disclose material that would identify particular people. I don't want any of my clients to ever worry—or hope—that their unique personal information will show up in my writing, so that they don't feel that there is an audience of readers in the session with us.

Because human growth and healing predates the advent of psychotherapy one hundred years ago, we have thousands of examples from the lives of heroes and heroines from literature, mythology, film, and fairy tales that demonstrate the processes of healing and growth. We'll utilize these stories as another way, a more imagistic and poetic way, to feel into these ten tools.

We'll also look at psychological research that indicates what may be most helpful in therapy. While there is no research that proves exactly what will work specifically for you, we do have studies that reveal psychological patterns that suggest effective directions for your work. The work of therapy involves a weaving together of heart and head, feeling and thinking. I hope to demonstrate this weaving in the content and process of the book, and that describing these tools from different angles will allow readers with different styles different ways to grasp and absorb the material.

YOUR THERAPIST'S ROLE

Your therapist's efforts *are* instrumental in activating your healing. Without her insight into what's happening unconsciously inside of you, her perception into what's going on in the back of your head, you could wander aimlessly for a long time. But ideally, through a combination of her training and her use of her personal experience of you, she can give you feedback about what may be going on unconsciously that causes you trouble.

While it may look like your therapist is just sitting there nodding her head, there's an awful lot of processing going on inside: processing both your feelings and the feelings she has about you, connecting your past with your present, and all the while watching not just what *is* said, but also what *isn't* said. Just as important as her insight is her empathy. Without it there would be little healing. Your therapist's understanding *and* personality interrupt your repetitive patterns in a way that frees you to try to live differently. It's not all your responsibility and you're not alone in the process.

THE TEMPO OF THERAPY

Deep, lasting change takes time to achieve, and this is true for just about everyone. It would be a rare individual who was able to do everything that I suggest in this book right away. Use of some of the tools I describe may come easily to you; others may feel very uncomfortable at first because they're unfamiliar and undeveloped. The challenge of learning these tools is no different from the challenges that determine the quality of our lives. And exploring what makes each of these tools difficult to use constitutes the work of psychotherapy. Finding your own tempo in using them is in itself an important part of the process. Further, please don't take these suggestions as "shoulds," or as hard-and-fast rules; take them rather as opportunities to enhance your work with your therapist when and as you are ready.

Psychotherapy is a very individual process. You may use some of these tools more than others, and you may use tools that I don't discuss in this book. My goal is not to be exhaustive or technical, but to be concise and clear, describing what is most often helpful to most clients in their efforts to grow. If you see these tools as possibilities rather than obligations, they will be much more beneficial to you.

The suggestions in this book are intended for people who want to make changes in their lives, changes in how they think, feel, and behave. Many people use therapy to sustain and support themselves in a difficult time, and do not set goals to make changes. For those of you in this situation, some of these tools may not apply. There is no harm in such an approach, but it would be best to clarify what your goals are with your therapist.

The type of therapy that I will describe tends to be long-term, though I've seen plenty of people get a great deal out of it in the first few months. Part of the reason I've written this book is so that your therapy doesn't go on longer than it needs to. But this doesn't mean I am suggesting that you sprint through the process or that we create another form of short-term therapy. Psychotherapy is not a drive-through activity: research suggests that longer treatment correlates with better outcome.[3] I suggest that you settle in and reside there for a while, rather than having one foot out the door, like a tourist ready to drive on to the next sight.

To use a different metaphor, I don't believe that we can fast-forward the process of psychotherapy. But I do think that learning what *you* can do in the process will help you to remove the "commercials," the periods when the therapeutic action seems stalled or irrelevant. The examples I've used in this book are by necessity all condensed; the process may appear to be on fast-forward, but actually takes some time.

WHAT TYPE OF THERAPY IS THIS ABOUT?

The tools that I describe here have proved their value in a wide variety of therapies used to help individual adults. The overarching term for this type of therapy is psychodynamic psychotherapy, which, on the face of it, would appear to be useless technical jargon. However, unpack it and it says a lot: psychodynamic refers to a mind or soul that's vigorous, purposeful, active, and changing. Part of that mind is unconscious—it's powerful but not easily seen. A therapy that is psychodynamic is one that works with this subterranean energy, and the therapeutic relationship, to bring about healing.

Included within this overarching field of psychodynamic psychotherapy are depth psychotherapy, insight-oriented therapy, expressive therapy, and psychoanalytic psychotherapy (Freudian, Jungian, interpersonal, object relations, and self-psychology). They are all designed to bring about lasting personality change by understanding unconscious processes, and by exploring what happens with the therapist in the sessions themselves. The tools in this book are drawn from the clinical wisdom accrued in over one hundred years of an evolving approach to self-understanding, healing, and growth that these therapies have honed.

While some of these tools are used in the newer forms of therapy known as cognitive and behavioral therapies, the tradition that I have drawn from is much less structured, and typically longer-term than cognitive and behavioral therapies. Cognitive and behavioral therapies tend to focus on the removal of specific symptoms, tend to be shorter-term, and include very specific instructions about the client's role.

The work I am describing in this book is holistic in that we work with the entire personality of the client, trying to understand root causes rather than focusing exclusively on symptoms such as anxiety or depression. It also tends to be "nondirective," personalized, and spontaneous; we don't impose a structure on the process, and we usually have the client begin the session. In cognitive and behavioral therapies there is less emphasis on unconscious process and the therapeutic relationship.

These tools may be used in work with psychologists, social workers, psychiatrists, nurses, and counselors, none of which are bound to a particular sort of therapy.

I briefly explore the decision of which type of therapy you might find most helpful in Appendix A: Starting Therapy, and briefly describe research demonstrating the efficacy of psychodynamic psychotherapy in Appendix C. My purpose in this book is not to argue the benefits of one type of therapy over another. However, I believe that this book will demonstrate the extensive benefits of a therapy that leaves enough time and space to use these ten tools flexibly and organically, that takes into account unconscious processes, and that uses the therapeutic relationship, all for deep, lasting change.

* * *

You may notice that the terms "healing" and "growth" are seldom seen separately in this book. The two belong together; healing leads to growth and growth leads to healing. I think that I can safely speak for many therapists that our hope for our clients is not just to remove a problem, but to move you beyond the problem to a more fulfilling way of living. The issues that bring people into therapy often lead them to more positive change than they had initially hoped for. I hope that this book makes that possible for you.

Chapter One:

Get Real: Take Off the Mask and Show Your Many Faces

"That's Eleanor. She's a fact checker."

> *"Do you talk to your therapist about this?"*
> *"Of course not, that's much too private."*
> —*Kissing Jessica Stein*

After his fourth combat tour, to Afghanistan in 2011, Sgt. First Class Michael B. Lube, a proud member of the Army Special Forces, came home alienated and angry. Once a rock-solid sergeant and devoted husband, he became sullen, took to drinking, got in trouble with his commanders, and started beating his wife.

"He would put this mask on, but behind it was a shattered version of the man I knew," said his wife, Susan Ullman.

She begged him to get help, but he refused, telling her: "I'll lose my security clearance. I'll get thrown out." When she quietly reached out to his superior officers for guidance, she said, she was told: "Keep it in the family. Deal with it."

And so he did. Last summer, just days after his 36th birthday, Sergeant Lube put on his Green Beret uniform and scribbled a note, saying, "I'm so goddamn tired of holding it together." Then he placed a gun to his head and pulled the trigger.

—*The New York Times,* June 6, 2014

BEWARE THE DANGERS OF THE "GOOD CLIENT" MASK

Let's start with the paradox right at the heart of psychotherapy: working too hard to be a "good" client will limit what you get out of it. If working hard means being compliant and taking in what your therapist says without question, you're in for a long, dry, and not very productive process. Working hard could mean different things to different people. But whatever it is that you think you're supposed to be doing in therapy, if you restrict yourself to it, your progress will certainly be limited. In fact, to make progress you may need to work harder at being a "bad" client.

Trying hard in therapy by doing only what you think you're supposed to be doing would be like wearing a mask in your session, a mask that shows only one face, one facet, of your personality. We all need to use masks in certain areas of our lives. Consciously choosing to present just one part of our personality, a particular mask, helps us to get along with others and to feel safe in the world.

While the most common mask is a polite one, we may also present ourselves as intimidating, cheery, rebellious, self-effacing, invulnerable, needy, detached, or superior, to name just a few of the ways that we prefer to appear at times. Masks aren't necessarily fake; ideally they are just limited expressions of who we are. How effective they are depends on whether they are appropriate to the situation. If the mask covers too much, or if we never take it off, our self-expression is quite narrow, which can lead to the problems that bring us into therapy. An appropriate mask has an important place in our lives—but that place isn't in therapy.

BRING ALL OF THE DIFFERENT PARTS OF YOUR PERSONALITY INTO YOUR SESSIONS

This paradox of working hard in therapy need not paralyze you: you need only to redefine what it means to work hard. Working hard in therapy includes taking off the mask and bringing in as many different parts of your personality as possible, not just the one facet of your personality that the mask shows. Some parts want to work hard and others want to just pout and complain. Others would like to play and others would like to cry. Don't worry, you're in good company: as Walt Whitman wrote, "I am large, I contain multitudes."

Let's not call these multitudes good or bad, let's see them all as part of who we are. Taking off the mask and bringing all of these aspects of ourselves into the room is part of what leads to healing and growth. Getting to know the different parts of our psychology, many of them that we've hidden from others and from ourselves, is part of what it means to work on ourselves in therapy. And, according to some research,[1] is what many clients find to be one of the most helpful aspects of the process.

Acknowledging these hidden parts of our personalities, sometimes undeveloped parts, and letting them show in session, may feel like a wound to our idealized sense of whom we want to be, but it's also how we move toward growth and wholeness. The masks we wear cut us off not just from others, but also from the possibilities of our own personalities, possibilities that can make life richer and more fulfilling.

PAY ATTENTION TO WHO IT IS THAT YOU WANT TO LEAVE OUT

Trying too hard to be a good client, or trying too hard to please the therapist, could be a repetition of what you've been doing for years, and it may hide the parts of you that you need to bring into your process. When you notice what you want to hold back from your therapist (your angry, childish, vulnerable, or strong parts, for instance), you get clues as to what you have excluded from your personality.

Whatever you think it means to be a good client will make for an interesting discussion with your therapist. Exploring with your therapist what you think you are supposed to do in therapy will tell you a lot about the issues that have kept you from living as you'd like to live. It might also be interesting to talk about what you'd love to do in therapy but think you shouldn't.

Sigmund Freud, the founder of psychoanalysis, encapsulated his belief in what work the patient needs to do in the Fundamental Rule: say whatever comes into mind, even if you think it unimportant or irrelevant or nonsensical or embarrassing or distressing. I don't recommend this technique, known as free association, for everyday interactions, but it is a helpful direction for work with your therapist.

In similar fashion, when your therapist asks you a question, don't censor or think about it too much. Say the first thing that pops into mind. You can always qualify it later. This approach opens the possibility for the many different aspects of your personality to come to the surface. The more you can do this in the here and now, describing your experience in the session itself, the more you will be able to work at deeper levels of your issues.

Rather than presenting only your mask—your social self—in session, you'll need to present the full range of your facial expressions, metaphorically speaking. Bring your mask in, show what it looks like, but then take it off and study it to see how it works and what it's covering up. This part that we want to cover up, deny, or get rid of, is known as the shadow, that part that we don't want to expose to the light. As we'll find out, the shadow causes problems only to the degree that it's hidden or unconscious; once we begin to integrate it more consciously, it actually enriches our personality.[2]

Cindy

Cindy was in her late twenties and was determined to study law and become an environmental attorney. She had come from a working-class family and had worked hard since her early teens not only to get good grades and develop a good resumé, but also to help bring some money into the family. She came to therapy at the suggestion of her boyfriend, who felt that while she didn't get demonstrably angry, she was too hard on herself, on him, and on everyone around them. Even though she tried to hide her anger, people could feel it.

In our first session she made it a point to let me know that her problems were not serious and that she was actually in pretty good shape. And she was clearly a strong person; since completing undergraduate school she was working two jobs to save money, ran marathons, and served on the rather contentious board of the local food co-op.

But Cindy was emotionally exhausted on a profound level and kept trying to hold back tears in our initial session. This wasn't her plan for therapy; she had intended to use her considerable willpower to blast through her problems with strength and determination.

At first she was baffled by what was happening, but she eventually allowed herself to acknowledge that she had been trying to ignore her emotional depletion and now wanted to hide it from me. She began to take her mask off. She imagined that I would think she was a weakling like everyone else who went to therapy. She liked to think of herself as having no limits, and any sign of limitations proved to her that she was weak and vulnerable. Tears, fatigue, and limitations didn't fit in with her mask.

While she was disturbed by her tears and exhaustion, she also had some sense that this more vulnerable side was an important aspect of herself that she needed to come to terms with—in one way or another.

The heroic identity her mask portrayed had truth to it—she did have some of the warrior in her personality and she was determined to make changes in the world. But to think of herself and to present herself in this exclusively heroic way denied other essential aspects of her personality—parts that needed downtime and play.

Cindy gained some awareness of these other parts in that first session, but it took time for her to become more comfortable with them and to actually accept them. In one session she adamantly expressed her disdain for weakness, hers and everyone else's. Then, somewhat surprised by her vehemence, she sat back in curiosity and wondered how she had become so judgmental.

She recalled that, accurately or not, she had felt loved by her father for her strength, and disregarded whenever she felt tired, sad, or discouraged. As we explored her relationship to him, it became clear that she had adopted the values she had thought he embraced, thinking it would win her his approval.

She went back and forth for some time about whether her "limitations" made her a weak person. It took courage for her to take off her mask, let her tears flow, and allow me to see what she was really going through. She told me about the times that she felt exhausted, and about the times when she really didn't feel like training for another marathon or going to another meeting. She admitted to me that at times she didn't feel like coming to her sessions because she felt that she was betraying her values.

Eventually Cindy came to accept that the oppressive way she treated herself was actually counterproductive. It led to her irritability, impatience, and exhaustion. She also came to understand that efforts to make herself "a better person" will backfire if they merely exclude unwanted parts of her personality, rather than get to know, understan d, and integrate those parts consciously.

AIM FOR WHOLENESS AND A TRUE SELF, NOT PERFECTION

The healthy human psyche seeks not perfection, but wholeness. Whatever chance we have for real, sustainable integrity comes about through unity and inclusion, integrating and balancing as many different parts of our psychology as we can, rather than excluding some of them because they don't fit into our idealized standard of perfection. The experience of wholeness is represented by the mandala, a venerated shape found in cultures across the globe that combines the opposite qualities of squareness and roundness, relating all the different and complementary parts to a center.

Here are two mandalas, one a classical religious representation, the other a very personal expression by mandala artist April Castoldi (on the right):

When we aspire to wholeness rather than to perfection we bring in all the different parts of ourselves into sessions: the part that is afraid this isn't going to work, the part that would rather skip the session today, and the part that thinks that no decent therapist could possibly hang such an ugly painting on her wall.

The idea of wholeness is similar to what is expressed by the phrase "the true self," our complete and authentic personality. Emotional health is achieved partly by finding a realistic way to live out the true self. Betraying the true self can lead to anxiety, depression, compulsion, suspiciousness, addiction, and relationship problems. In therapy we can observe how we betray our true selves in both conscious and unconscious ways.

I will address these more in Chapter Two when we discuss emotions, but as a brief example of how you might consciously betray your true self, you may notice yourself thinking, "Maybe I don't have to tell my therapist about that episode that happened yesterday that I'm not so proud of." Yes, it's true, you *don't* have to tell him or her *anything*, but why don't you want to, and what part of you are you hiding if you don't talk about it? Ask yourself: Who wants to hide it, who is it that is being hidden, and who wants to tell about it?

The famous British psychoanalyst D. W. Winnicott once worked with a patient who had previously been in psychoanalysis with another analyst for years. The patient told Winnicott that his therapeutic work had really started only when Winnicott recognized that he had existed only falsely, and that all of the work he had previously done in analysis had been done on a false self that the previous analyst mistook for the true self.[3] Watch to see whether you bring your true self or your false self into session; distinguishing between the two can be enormously helpful.

Our experiences in life often force us to split ourselves into two halves, one supposedly good, the other supposedly bad. Here's a story about reuniting the different parts that have been at odds.

The Cloven Viscount Is Reunited

In *The Cloven Viscount*, a novella by Italo Calvino,[4] a man goes to war and is torn in half by a cannonball. His two halves are saved and rehabilitated, but separately; the right side is helped by military physicians, the left side by spiritual hermits. These two halves then live very separate lives for years.

The right half returns to his castle in Italy and terrorizes everyone by cutting objects and people into half. "The Bad 'Un," as this half is later called, believes that being cut in half and suffering enlightened him, and he believes that everyone else should be torn in half too, because "beauty and knowledge and justice exists only in what has been torn to shreds."

The left half, known as "The Good 'Un," has compassion for everyone, and tries to do good, but is rather naïve and righteous in his crusades. His efforts at good sometimes don't end so well. He becomes moralistic and forbids the celebrations that had helped many to survive. While he isn't as ostensibly destructive as the "The Bad 'Un," he's also cold-hearted in his own way.

It seems that the separation has caused each of them to go to extremes.

Eventually they both end up back in the village they came from, and they both want to marry the same woman, Pamela, who lives a simple life enjoying nature and animals. She interrupts their one-sided ways of living; they see her wholeness, sense what's missing in their lives, and set their sights on getting it back—through her. Each one woos her in his own awkward way. "The Bad 'Un" insists that he must, and will, have her and keep her in the tower of the castle (where of course he can split her from nature). "The Good 'Un" tries to civilize her, reading spiritual texts to her and urging her to join him in his acts of righteousness. He tells her, "Doing good together is the only way to love." She replies suggestively, "A pity. I thought there were other ways."

At a loss as to what to do, Pamela tells them both that she'll marry them, and manages to get them both to show up for the wedding at the same time and place. A fight ensues, and the two halves are both wounded, their sides opened and bleeding once again. The village doctor rushes in and takes the opportunity to sew the two sides together. The Viscount is whole once again.

The conflicts we face in life can, as with the Viscount, lead to splits in our personality, cutting us off from valuable character traits. Sometimes this happens when we're young, before we've become aware of these characteristics. These splits can wreck our balance and rob us of our wholeness. The wounds that bring us into therapy often serve as opportunities to bring all the conflicted parts back into the room to be united and healed again.

EXPAND YOUR COMFORT ZONE WITH YOUR THERAPIST

Therapy is not a solitary endeavor. Getting real *with* your therapist, taking off the mask with another person, is part of what makes therapy effective. It's just not the same in the privacy of your living room. This interpersonal aspect of therapy is also part of what makes it transformational rather than a loose string of interesting ideas that you quickly forget.

Taking off the mask with your therapist may bring into focus a discrepancy between who you think you want to be or should be, and who you really are. It could make you feel uncomfortable, and that isn't necessarily bad. Therapy is most effective when there are periods of mild to moderate stress.[5] If your work with your therapist is too comfortable, little change will occur. By gently exposing yourself to the situation that you fear, showing aspects of your personality that you had hidden before (for instance, the part that's proud, insecure, lazy, or provocative), you can increase your comfort with that part of you and begin to feel more at ease with it in the outside world. Think of it as expanding your comfort zone.

Some behavioral therapies successfully treat anxiety by incrementally exposing the anxious person to the very thing that he or she fears. For instance, people who are afraid of germs and so wash their hands dozens, if not hundreds, of times a day, are gradually exposed to the things that trigger their anxiety and then told to stand at the sink and not wash their hands. Eventually, exposure to the thing they fear actually changes their brains and they no longer feel the compulsion to wash. Psychotherapy also uses exposure in a beneficial way, gently exposing us to the aspects of relationships that we fear the most, which for many includes being authentic.

Some clients want to come in and tell their therapist about all the progress they've made that week and leave it at that. I remember when I first began psychotherapy as a client, I felt that a good session was one in which I could report lots of progress and "good" behavior on my part to the therapist (for instance, that I debated a teacher, I said no to a project that would drain me, or I didn't obsess about a bad performance). I suspect that that was what I needed to do at the time. But eventually I realized that it was discovering my weaker places, the discrepancies between how I wanted to look to the therapist and who I actually was, that helped me to make more progress. Your therapist does need to know what progress you're making, and positive feedback is certainly helpful, but if you don't allow your therapist to also see the places where you're still struggling, her help is limited to support.

Many clients have told me that one of the things they want to accomplish in therapy is to become comfortable living in their own skin, in effect not having to wear their mask all the time. Learning to live in your own skin requires an environment where you feel free to be authentic. Ideally our families provide this early on in life, but some of us never had this, and instead felt that we needed to create a mask either to protect ourselves from others or to get along with them. For most of us, it's not so easy to simply wake up one morning and with an exertion of willpower take off the mask. Therapy presents an opportunity to try out being in your own skin gradually. This is an incremental process that you can engage in at your own tempo.

"But what if I'm a very private person?" Some people don't feel comfortable revealing the more personal details of their lives to their therapist right away, if at all. You should not feel rushed. But it will be important to explain these feelings to your therapist at some point so that the two of you can work together to both respect your needs and understand them. The process may need to be very gradual for you.

ON NEEDING AND NOT NEEDING TO BE LIKED

At the same time, trying to be indifferent to what your therapist thinks of you could also limit your progress. While it might seem like it would liberate you from compliance or convention not to care about what your therapist thinks, carried to extremes trying not to care could actually cause more problems than it solves. You might just be wearing a different sort of mask. We have evolved as social animals, and needing to be liked enough to be part of the tribe has been highly adaptive for our survival as a species. Trying to get rid of something so deeply ingrained in us is extremely difficult, if not foolhardy. You could spend your entire life in therapy trying not to need to be liked and never fully succeed.

The problem is not so much that we want to be liked, but that we might betray our true self to be liked by everyone. Nature has created us as unique, individual beings with distinctive contributions to make. If, out of a fear of not being liked, we don't fulfill that uniqueness, we may experience feelings of emptiness, meaninglessness, and depression.

A more effective goal is to honor your true self with its unique capacities, and not to betray it, but to find its place in the world. Wanting to be liked for who you are authentically is quite human. But if you betray yourself by cutting out parts of your wholeness to fit in or to be liked, you will prohibit a flow within yourself that is necessary for emotional health. You probably won't be able to get everyone to like your true self, but you need acceptance from only a relatively small number of people to feel fulfilled. You may want to ask yourself, "What do I really need to have seen and validated by my therapist? Is that authentic to me, or is it an artificial version that I've tried to create to get approval?"

DISCOVERING UNCONSCIOUS AREAS: OPEN THE DOOR TO UNDISCOVERED ROOMS

So far what I've described refers to *conscious* attempts to use a mask to hide parts of your personality from your therapist and others. But there may be other parts of your psychology that you exclude without knowing it. You may not necessarily reject these other parts intentionally, but rather you may never have known they were there to include; you've never had access to them before. A fairly common theme in dreams is discovering rooms in our house or apartment that we didn't know were there. These rooms represent parts of ourselves that we had been unaware of, not necessarily parts that we had tried to avoid, but parts that have not been accessible before.

The integration of these other rooms, these other parts of your personality, begins with an openness to your therapist's suggestions that these rooms exist, and an openness to her ideas about what they might symbolize. These are parts that you may need a mirror to start seeing, an outside source that will reflect back these parts that you can't see directly, some of them beautiful, some of them not so pretty.

If you find yourself quickly rejecting something your therapist suggests (for instance, that you're angry, passive, creative, or overly suspicious), that could be an indication that there is a disturbing truth there—something about you is about to be exposed, and it makes you anxious. If you can slow down, put judgment aside, and really consider the idea or observation that's being offered, you may find that it leads you to an *"aha"* moment. Some things that never made sense before will finally start to come together as you open the door to that other room.

None of us enter or leave therapy with total knowledge of our psyche; there will always be parts of it to be discovered. But the more we can be open to acknowledging all the different parts of our personality, not letting shame crowd them out, the bigger our psychological house will be, and the more psychological space we have to live in.

You may be tempted to object: "If something is unconscious, then how could I possibly become aware of it?" Good question. But the entire therapeutic process is about making the unconscious conscious, and that isn't as conveniently impossible as it might seem. The lines between conscious and unconscious aren't so distinct, or so impermeable.

Currently, one of the most exciting developments in neurological research is how flexible and adaptive the brain is; with the right processes it can be rewired to some extent.[6] At times your therapist may suggest that there might be something going on inside of you without your knowing it, and with some openness on your part the *aha* happens, the moment when something you were unconscious of before comes into awareness as it resonates with what your therapist has suggested. Your brain literally changes as new neural connections are made, and your capacity for authenticity expands. Or, put differently, you are reunited with parts of yourself that you had been separated from.

SUMMARY

1. Don't try to be a "good patient" by wearing any particular mask.
2. Take off your mask and let all of the different parts of your personality come into session.
3. Pay attention to whom and what you want to leave out of session.
4. Aim for wholeness, not perfection.
5. Use your relationship with your therapist as a place to gradually expand your comfort zone.
6. It's OK to want to be liked, but don't betray your true self to do so.
7. Be open to acknowledging previously unknown parts of yourself.

Chapter Two:

Channel the Flow of Emotion:
Have Your Feelings without Your Feelings Having You

"Could we up the dosage? I still have feelings."

"The wise man is as a guest-house, and he admits all the thoughts that occur to him, whether of joy or of sorrow, with the same welcome, knowing that, like Abraham, he may entertain angels unawares. . . Let grief as well as joy lodge in the heart, for grief is sent for our benefit as well as joy."

—Rumi, translated by E. H. Whinfield, MA

"Men are admitted into Heaven not because they have curbed & govern'd their Passions or have No Passions, but because they have Cultivated their Understandings."

—William Blake

The success of your work in therapy will hinge largely on how you treat your feelings in session. But there's a lot of confusion out there about just what this entails.

Does venting frustrations help? How about crying? Should I exercise my ability to stand back objectively and be rational about my problems? Or should I try to purge my anger by expressing my feelings about my parents, my boss, my spouse, or the health insurance representative who denied my claim?

Many people have gotten the impression that therapy works by getting rid of disturbing feelings through venting or catharsis. Others think that if they can maintain distance from their feelings, they'll achieve change through insight and intellectual understanding. Both of these play an important role in therapy, but, used exclusively, the benefits of either one are limited. In fact, used alone, neither of these approaches truly values feeling. While some venting, for example through tears, anger, or simple expressions of frustration, may be helpful, and understanding problems through insight is helpful, more substantial change comes about in therapy from a deeper process that's not just about getting rid of something unpleasant or rising above it intellectually. Rather, it's about receiving feeling and using it wisely.

For the sake of clarity I'll describe this process in three steps:

1. Allow feeling to rise from deep inside so that it can be expressed and heard.
2. Contain it in consciousness, without reacting to it impulsively, so that you can know it well.
3. Direct the energy and wisdom gained from the awareness of that feeling.

I will refer to this as channeling emotion. In therapy we engage feeling and let it flow into consciousness, but we also contain and explore it, reflecting on what it has to tell us, so that we can skillfully channel the energy that it offers. Our emotions are both informing and transforming, but leaving out any of these steps may keep us from utilizing their benefits.

This process isn't just a one-time thing, but rather a pattern that we repeat enough times so that it becomes second nature, almost like a dance. The rhythm of these steps may be fast, a quick turnaround between expression, containing, and direction that takes only seconds. But it could also take on a slower rhythm, requiring months or, in some cases, even years after the first expressions before the directing begins. Eventually the three steps don't feel so separate, but part of a fluid movement in response to the music within.

Your individual psychology will determine which part of this process you need to work on developing most. Some children were responded to only when they expressed their emotions dramatically or impulsively, leading to tendencies to exaggerate and discharge emotions in unhealthy ways. Others were rewarded for controlling their emotions, and may end up restricting the flow too much. In therapy we connect past experience with present experience to understand the strategies we've enlisted to express or control our emotions, and to exercise better ways of handling them, so that we have them, rather than them having us.

Imagine that you have an emotional dimmer switch, just about where your chest meets your neck, that controls the flow of feelings and ideas that rise up from your gut into your head. Imagine that the feeling and ideas that come from your gut provide lots of useful information. Early on, as a child, you had some nascent capacity to use this switch: when feelings, ideas, and images were painful, you turned it down; when they felt good, you opened it up.

What would it be like if after a while, things got too intense and rather than develop this facility, you just turned it off completely, lost track of the switch, and forgot that it existed? You'd be left without your best source of wisdom about yourself and how to handle life. Or imagine that the switch broke and you could never turn it off, leaving you with a never-ending torrent of intense information that you couldn't process.

One of the ways that therapy helps is to get that switch working again, and working better than it did before. But it's not so easy. It may take courage to let the feelings in, and it may take restraint not to get carried away or overwhelmed by them. In effect we're learning to adjust and direct the flow of emotion without stopping it completely. Over time we realize that even if it feels bad, it's important to listen to the messages. But we also need to be savvy about how and when to use this switch: less open when you have a difficult presentation to make (whatever your gut has to say, it can wait), and more open when you're with someone on a first date (so that you take in what your gut is trying to tell you about this person).

Therapy provides a unique setting in which we can develop our relationship with emotions, trying new ways of handling them so that when we go out into the world we have a better sense of how to use them. You could consider therapy a dress rehearsal. Even the best improvising musicians spend hours a day honing their skills so that when it's time for the gig they're completely fluent with their instrument.

One reason that the exploration of feelings is so important is that we have layers of feeling, and the lower layers may not be obvious at first. For instance, you might be aware of your anger at your friend for canceling dinner plans (again), but not the fear, sadness, or even guilt that is underneath it. The arrangement of layers may also be reversed; you may be aware of fear, sadness, or guilt when your friend cancels, but not the anger beneath. And dramatic displays of anxiety may actually cover far more than they show. Excavating to the deepest level will help you to live your life in a more conscious way, rather than react to feelings that you're not aware of. In therapy we watch for sequences of feelings in the session itself to see what the primary emotion is and how you typically respond to it.

I'll discuss the why and the how of this tool by describing the sequence of expressing, containing, and directing emotion, but the division is really only one of convenience, as they're not so separate. In practice this process is far more natural than the division may imply. My hope is that by explaining this tool in very slow motion, watching it frame by frame, I'll help you to see how you can use therapy to develop a better relationship with your emotions.

Perhaps worse than not extracting the wisdom, direction, and energy that emotions can offer us, is missing out on the enormous pleasure they can bring if they are either inaccessible or overwhelming. Keeping out the bad ones also keeps out the good ones. Regaining access to the ones that bring pleasure is in itself worth the effort.

EXPRESSING FEELING

This first step, allowing feelings to rise up and come into consciousness spontaneously, is usually relatively simple, using words to describe what we're experiencing:

- I was nervous about coming to session today.
- My son made me extremely angry yesterday.
- I felt really proud of my work on that project.

But expressing feelings that are out of our comfort zone may not be so easy:

- I feel like I should be more generous. I really hate it when people ask me to give them things or do things for them.
- My illness has caused me to be incontinent and I feel intense shame about it.
- I'm really disappointed that you can't understand me more easily.

There could be many reasons that this gets difficult; in addition to the feeling itself that we need to express, we may also have feelings such as a fear that we would be getting messy and out of control, or becoming vulnerable or indulgent, if we were to express certain feelings. Working on this begins with an awareness of being blocked, and continues with an exploration of the cause of the blockage and discomfort. We challenge the assumptions behind those blockages, questioning our old ideas about why we feel it's not acceptable to even acknowledge certain feelings, much less express them. Then gently, gradually, and courageously we take the chance to push past our comfort zone by giving voice to the things that make us uneasy or distressed. Practicing this with your therapist eventually opens your channel.

An increasing number of studies indicate that the more intense varieties of forced catharsis that had been in vogue twenty or thirty years ago in therapy may actually deepen the ruts of agitation and rumination that we hope to escape.[1] We could think of that as trying to pump feelings rather than channel their natural flow.

But at the same time, any therapy that's going to have a lasting effect on us needs to engage us emotionally.[2] If we don't engage emotionally we leave parts of our brain and our personality disconnected from the process, a disconnecting that repeats a failed strategy of splitting off parts of our psyche rather than uniting them. What we need in therapy is an accepting recognition and judicious use of the feelings we do have, not an attempt to force feelings we don't have.

For instance, crying doesn't always leave us feeling better. But studies[3] support what we've known and practiced intuitively in therapy for decades—crying in the presence of someone who is supportive, and coming to understand what underlies the crying, can help us to feel better. If you suffer from major depression or an anxiety disorder, repeated crying may not make you feel better.[4] The take-home on what to do in therapy is that it can be very helpful to allow yourself to cry in session if it feels like you're connecting to something important within, because you're in a safe place where the feelings can arise and be understood.

Acknowledging the pain of childhood, for instance, is a liberating and necessary step for many; if tears come naturally, and if they release something deep inside, let them flow. But trying to force yourself to cry may not be helpful. If you notice yourself holding back tears, that would be important to tell your therapist, and, hopefully, let them flow eventually.

On the other hand, if it feels like crying is just repeating what you're always doing anyway, it may be helpful to stand back and understand what needs to be heard and seen that hasn't been acknowledged yet.

In the case of anger, experiencing and expressing it in session and then trying to understand it may be informative and empowering, but the mere process of expressing it does not by itself usually lead to real transformation. Not to mention that a perennial dwelling in anger can increase your risk of heart disease.

How you work with anger in therapy will vary depending on the sources of your anger—for instance, whether you've been abused,[5] or whether you just haven't accepted that things aren't always going to go the way you believe they should. If you've been the victim of trauma, it may be helpful to mobilize anger to empower yourself. But if your anger arises more from not getting your way, rage and frustration would call for curiosity about why such circumstances push your buttons, and for developing the capacity to contain your anger. As psychoanalyst Willard Gaylin[6] wrote, the problem for some people is not so much their inability to release anger, as it is their "unlimited capacity to generate unwarranted anger."

In all cases it's important to acknowledge anger, and then either channel the energy or let it go. Developing the ability to say, "That makes me really angry" is a great tool when we're able to talk to someone about how he or she made us angry, and much more effective than throwing a bowl of hot tomato soup. But there are other circumstances when we can't be direct, and eventually we need to find a place to direct that energy (for example, as MADD, Mothers Against Drunk Driving, have done) or release it, through acceptance. Indulging or holding onto anger can cause emotional and physical problems. Forgiveness can be helpful for you, if and when you are ready.

But it's also possible to be too controlling of your feelings. Some clients feel more comfortable being abstract and intellectual in therapy, focusing on why they are the way they are, leaving out the actual experience of feelings. While we might like to think that we can be completely rational and conscious creatures, to try to be entirely reasonable actually robs us of experiences that make life ful-filling. Understanding the origins of our personal psychology is an important step, but we need to take that as a second step, after we've allowed ourselves to hold the emotions that have led us to where we are and the current feelings that we experience. In fact, staying in an intellectual mode is often a defense against feeling. Intellectual facility is a great skill to have, but we don't want it to have you either.

To Suppress or to Repress

None of this is to say that we have to maintain all these feelings in consciousness all the time. Many people have the impression that they should somehow always be living in complete awareness of all their feel-ings all the time, which is a good way to drive yourself completely bonkers.

While I usually try not to use jargon, this is one subject where I think that the clarification of a couple of psychological terms will be helpful, partially because these terms have entered the mainstream in a confusing way, and partially because it helps me to make an important distinction. The terms repression and suppression are often used interchangeably, as if they refer to the same process, but they don't.

Repression occurs when a feeling or event is too disturbing to let it into consciousness; we forget or ignore the feeling without being aware of doing so. We may repress uncomfortable feelings of love or hate because they're too disturbing, and in the process develop mal-adaptive coping strategies without being aware of it. So, for instance, if early in life you repressed feelings of affection because you felt that your parents were uncomfortable with them, you may continue to block possibilities of love later in life without knowing it.

Suppression, on the other hand, occurs when we consciously choose not to focus on something. So, for instance, you may be fascinated by Brad Pitt or Angelina Jolie, but you wisely decide not to fuel cravings for them because you probably won't get the chance to even meet them, much less do anything really tasty with them.

Both repression and suppression have their benefits at appropriate times and in appropriate doses. But while repression is only a necessary evil that takes over of its own accord when feelings are intolerable, suppression is often a very helpful tool, as it allows us to decide what to keep in consciousness and what to consciously push to the side so that we can get on with life.

So please don't imagine that you have to hold all of this information in consciousness all the time. But, don't bypass the first step of letting it rise into consciousness in the first place.

Engaging the Missing or Indistinct Emotions

But at times it may feel like there's nothing to suppress anyway, no conscious reluctance to feel an emotion and nothing that wants to rise from your gut through that channel into your head, just a complete blank at the idea of accessing emotions. Emotions may seem nonexistent or so faint that you can't hear their message, and it may seem impossible to become conscious of something that's never been conscious. How can we connect with something that was repressed years ago? I'll have more to say about this in Chapter Three, but for now consider that the barrier between conscious and unconscious is not as impermeable as you might think, and that therapy is designed explicitly to help information cross over this barrier.

In cases like these, when feelings may actually have been repressed unknowingly years ago, you'll need to dive deep inside to retrieve them. But that deep dive may take working in a manner that's different and more subtle than you're used to. You may need to sit quietly and listen carefully in order to tune in. The radio signal may seem very faint. Take your time to find the best channel for receptivity. If your therapist asks you how you feel, don't say, "I don't know" too quickly.

Eugene Gendlin, a professor of psychology at the University of Chicago, looked closely at the research that demonstrates the importance of the role of the client in psychotherapy, and concluded that many clients don't know how to use psychotherapy and never learn it, even if they spend years in therapy. After years of his own research he developed a series of six steps that together constitute what he believes to be the essential tool in psychotherapy: "focusing." He believes that these six steps lead not only to contact with emotion, but a felt shift in one's psychological well-being. I have condensed and summarized them here, but you can read his original descriptions on his website (www.focusing.org). He suggests that we:

1. Clear a space. Slow down and notice all of your present concerns as you experience them in your body.
2. Choose one of these concerns and notice the felt sense of it.
3. Develop a "handle" for the concern: let a word or phrase that describes the issue come to mind from the felt sense.
4. See if the handle resonates with the felt sense.
5. Ask what it is about the concern that gives it its particular quality and intensity. Ideally this will create a shift in your experience of the issue.
6. Receive this with friendly acceptance.

Gendlin emphasizes that it's essential that you achieve a direct, bodily "felt sense" of what needs recognition and change in your life, and that you experience it from within rather than merely accept your therapist's interpretation. What you're aiming for is a knowing similar to the sort of knowing that you're hungry from within the body, rather than deducing that you must be hungry because you haven't eaten for six hours.

CONTAINING FEELING

Developing the skill of experiencing emotion without avoiding it or impulsively acting on it is what author and psychologist Daniel Goleman[7] refers to as the master aptitude of emotional intelligence. In a way, reacting to a feeling, rather than observing it, is really just another more dramatic way of avoiding it, trying to get away from it by getting it over with. But it doesn't go away so easily. Reacting may deepen the ruts and increase the vehemence of the feeling rather than develop the capacity to hold it. Both being able to have a feeling without reacting to it, and being able to contain a feeling without controlling it, will help your progress enormously.

One of the ways that we learn to contain feelings is to label them. Using words to identify experience gives us a healthy distance from them without avoiding them. Doing so increases the activity of the left prefrontal cortex, the part of the brain that's more verbal, analytical, and logical, and lessens the activity of the amygdala, the part of the brain that's largely responsible for anxiety. One of the original functions of the amygdala was to allow us to deal immediately with dangers such as predators. But in the twenty-first century it often just leads us to scan anxiously and constantly for pachyderms and pythons, which most of us don't run into very often. Labeling the feeling—"Oh, it's that pachyderm fear again"—requires us to slow down and observe, and it gives us some perspective on the feeling without ignoring or denying it.

When we use words to bring our feelings into therapy, we engage different parts of the brain simultaneously and create new neural connections between the more emotional parts and the more rational parts. But this requires our efforts both to let feelings flow, and to control that flow as needed. The idea is to channel feeling rather than to either block it or propel it aimlessly.

So here's an optimal flow of emotion: you let it come up, you become aware of it, you sit with it, you get to know it, and you get more comfortable with it. But that doesn't mean that you wallow in it or that you necessarily act on it. To return to the "switch" metaphor, rather than turning off the upward flow of feelings from the gut at the throat before it can even get into the head, you need to let it rise farther up, into the head, where it can come into consciousness and you can hang out with it for a while before you decide what to do about it. In therapy we exercise the combination of flow and channeling by speaking our feelings before we decide to act on them. The idea is to make conscious decisions about what to do with feeling rather than have unconscious reactions.

Some people feel a need to express their emotions intensely. While this may be natural and have its benefits, if it feels compulsive, or if it feels pressured and unremitting, it will be important to step back and look at what may be going on inside. Ask yourself whether it feels like there is something you need your therapist to feel or understand that isn't being felt or understood. Sometimes our early life circumstances lead us to amplify our emotions in order to be heard, to gain respect, or to get whatever it is we need. What can also happen is that eventually you feel that just *expressing* emotions intensely isn't enough; you may come to believe on some unconscious level that you actually need to amplify and *feel* them more intensely for anyone to get it. This is a painful strategy, which may not be obvious at first. But with some focus on what's happening in sessions, it can be changed.

Fairy tales and mythology are filled with stories of heroes and heroines who are faced with the decision of whether to help, befriend, or marry an animal, often ones that aren't so attractive. Early in the story they often encounter animals that they decide to help out in some way. Later, when things are really impossible for the hero or heroine, the animals that they helped come back to return the favor, and help them overcome their challenges. In other fairy tales the maiden marries a frog who turns out to be a prince. Or the prince marries an ugly old woman who turns out to be a princess.

If you take these stories literally you're in for big trouble. Rescuing an animal may be a benevolent and satisfying thing to do; just don't imagine they'll morph into the partner of your dreams. On the other hand, if you understand these animals as representing your own instinctual emotions that will help you once you befriend them, *once you allow them to rise into consciousness*, they can offer you wisdom, energy, and companionship that make life more fulfilling. Staying completely in your head and turning away your instincts when they need your attention eventually leaves you disconnected from inner resources that would otherwise enable you to handle challenges that come your way and live a more gratifying life.

Belle Befriends Her Emotions

Belle's story from *Beauty and the Beast* serves as a good example of how we can relate to an emotion that seems dreadful to us at first, and as an example of how to contain an emotion before acting on it.

Belle is the prototypical Good Girl. She's polite, dutiful, generous, uncomplaining, and respectful. To save her father from being imprisoned by the Beast, she substitutes herself to live in a huge castle with the Beast. The Beast is ugly and uncouth at first, but she tolerates him. She speaks to him, reads with him, and even dances with him. Eventually, with her help, his social skills improve and she befriends him. But she won't marry him. She leaves the castle to visit her father, and when she's away she's able to see the Beast's suffering through the magic looking glass he's given her. Paradoxically, once she has some distance from him she's able to really see his anguish and empathize with him. At this point she rushes back to the castle to tell him that she loves him—the spell is broken and the beast transforms into a prince.

Similarly, in therapy we spend time with emotions that may be unattractive to us, but as we get to know them they transform. We understand why they are the way they are and with some distance we may even get to see what it feels like to live without them. Once we do that we have a real relationship with our emotions and their true form emerges, free of the spells that have been cast by the struggles we have encountered in life. Transformed, they become life partners rather than enemies.

DIRECTING FEELING

In therapy we make friends with our emotions and we listen carefully to them to see what they have to offer us. They have a profound role in our lives; they give us information about danger and safety, pleasure, direction, and a sense of what's truly valuable—without them we'd be wandering aimlessly,[8] and we might even question whether it's worth wandering at all. But it often happens that we aren't certain what a particular emotion has to tell us, and in some cases we may have lost track entirely of how to follow the direction, purpose, and message of any emotions.

When we know what an emotion is for, that emotional energy can flow into the right place. So, for instance, Cindy, the determined young woman I wrote about in Chapter One, wanted to dismiss her tears and sadness when they came up in the first session. But eventually she listened to what they had to tell her: she had become too identified with a heroic ideal and she needed to use some of her energy to nurture herself, to take time to slow down, reassess her values, and recharge. Part of her was crying out for relief from her oppressive way of living. Even if an emotion is causing you trouble, you can regard it as a signal, an early warning system, that tells you that there's something that you need to pay attention to.

But while emotions have played a central role in our survival as a species, giving us directions that have helped us to adapt and survive, some emotions don't seem to offer a particular direction for us to follow. In these cases we may need to think in terms of signals, rather than messages. I'll explain the difference.

Because Nature has given more priority to the quantity of our survival (live long enough to pass on as many copies of your genes as possible), it has placed less concern on the quality of our survival (how you feel isn't so important as long as you live long enough to pass on your genes). So for instance, Nature has been very generous with anxiety genes, and some of us have gotten more than our fair share of them. The result is that some of us are left with a perpetual state of worry, rather than with cues for particular dangers that we need to be aware of. This means that to find our direction and to feel more comfortable we may need to learn to recognize which are messages that give us direction and which are signals that indicate that old neurological by-products are in operation and causing us distress for no real reason.

Ask yourself: Does my anxiety communicate something specific that I need to attend to, or is this an old tape that keeps playing no matter what the circumstance? In a situation where an old irrelevant tape keeps playing, the persistence of the anxiety is more of a signal that the emotion is "off" or misleading, rather than a message of a danger that we need to attend to; it is a signal that we need to question the feeling we're experiencing. Yes, it's that pachyderm thing again.

THE ROLE OF THE EGO

But who is this who has or is had by these feelings? If I am not my emotions, who am I? We tend to experience ourselves through what we call the ego, not the ego of conceit, but the ego that serves an executive function and helps negotiate between feelings and the real world. Somebody needs to be calling the shots for this collection of different personality parts and feelings that we're comprised of. But it would be a mistake to think that the one calling the shots is the only one with value.

Imagine yourself as a small town for a moment. The ego ideally serves as a good mayor, listens to the citizens (the different emotions and personality parts) and everyone on the council, and then does what needs to be done for the betterment of all. Without an ego-mayor we have the garden club making decisions about the school system and the motorcycle club deciding which water filtration plant to purchase. On the other hand, if the ego-mayor takes too much control she becomes a despot. The ego-mayor is not the city, she just has a particular role to play in that city. She makes sure that all of its citizens are heard, takes into account their needs and desires, and effectively engages the energy that each citizen brings to the town. The mayor doesn't dictate, but tries to facilitate the greatest good for the greatest number of people by helping them to live and work together harmoniously. The mayor realizes that she is not the only citizen, but a citizen with a specific function.

To extend the metaphor just a bit, there are some citizens (some signals) that the mayor needs to hear but not follow. It's important to recognize and express feelings, but it isn't always such a good idea to believe that all of your feelings are accurate, or that we should always take their lead. For instance, it is important to acknowledge that at times you *feel* like everyone at your office hates you, but to believe that feeling as if it were accurate isn't always helpful. It's good to acknowledge that you *feel* like having an affair is the solution to all of your problems, but believing that feeling without questioning it is not so helpful. And you may be so anxious that you *feel* like you are about to be attacked by a lion or tiger, but don't believe it's true. The ego serves a role in sorting out feelings from beliefs so that we aren't misled by particularly intense feelings. In the next chapter we'll explore how to look inside and understand some of these intense feelings on a more symbolic level, rather than taking them as literal fact.

Therapy serves as a workout session for the ego: we strengthen the ego by containing feelings and using their energy appropriately so that it can do its job better. Here is an example of how this can look in psychotherapy:

Eric

Eric, a forty-two-year-old father of two who worked in technical support at a large law firm, had come to therapy for depression and to get help dealing with his anger. He was furious about the new schedule that had been set up at his job. It threw a huge proverbial wrench into the carefully scheduled arrangement of drop-off and retrieval that he and his wife had worked out to get their kids to their various activities. At a previous job he'd given his boss a piece of his mind when a similar schedule change had been imposed. Apparently it was the wrong piece of his mind because he was unceremoniously fired. Eric had no problem letting anger flow; in fact it flowed a little too easily, but there were other layers of feelings that weren't being attended to.

After we spoke about his job situation for a while, I could see that he was getting more agitated and it didn't seem like continuing to vent was helping him. In order to make more effective use of these feelings by enlisting his ego, I asked him to describe what it was like to get so angry, and to tell me where he felt it in his body. He sat back a bit on the couch and slowed down. This was different.

He usually focused on the content of his anger, what he was angry about, but not the experience of it, what it actually felt like to be angry. He had a channel open for it, but he hadn't known how to contain it and study it. He told me that he felt strength and power in his arms and hands, but that in his midsection there was a sense of being tense, shaky, uncomfortable, and scared. He took a few deep breaths and I could see him switching gears. As he observed his body, he was able to contain his anger, feeling it without being overwhelmed by it.

Eric started to describe and label the many layers of feelings that were manifest in these different reactions in his body, including not only anger, but also fear and sadness that he hadn't wanted to acknowledge. He spoke first about his fear of not being able to offer his kids everything that he wanted to, a fear of inadequacy that haunts many men in their role as providers. He spoke about his anger at himself for not getting his life together earlier, leaving him struggling to create the life he wanted. He was upset with himself for the way he had scheduled his own life, waiting until thirty-five to get a regular salaried position.

But he was also angry at his parents for the way they had scheduled him: a childhood crammed with activities designed to get him into a good college. In his twenties and early thirties he had rebelled and made it a point to have no one telling him that he had to be anywhere or do anything at a particular time. The feelings he had in his body reflected his conflict about living autonomously; he felt the anger about being controlled in his arms, but also his fears of being inadequate in his gut.

As he spoke about his history he also became aware of a deep sadness about what had not happened in his life, things he had missed that could never be made up. His anger had been one way he tried to avoid feeling this sadness. But now he let this, too, flow into consciousness where it could melt away some of the severity that had built up. By allowing all of these feelings into consciousness and then containing them, he exercised and strengthened his ego.

Eric did have reason to be angry, and the message of the anger was important, but the way he had handled his anger in the past, both passively aggressive and directly aggressive, hadn't been very productive. Feeling what it did to his body, his state of mind, and his outer situation all gave him motivation to try to handle it in a different way, to channel that energy more effectively.

We discussed how he could present his case to his supervisor at work and arrange a schedule that worked for everyone there. But more importantly, he began to understand the sources of his anger, both old and new, and to find a way to use the determination that the anger offered him, rather than to have the anger use him.

In the weeks that followed we were able to expand our understanding of the themes that were inherent in his anger, and what they meant about how to live his life. The anger also indicated a deep discontent about the severe control that he inflicted on himself. Through our repeated exploration of this theme, he became able to notice when he was about to impose brutal self-discipline, and choose to treat himself with more respect.

THE PRICE OF ADDICTIVE BEHAVIOR

"Our lives are mostly a constant evasion of ourselves."
—T. S. Elliot

A very succinct, though somewhat simplistic, definition of therapy would explain it as a process that helps us to stop avoiding the feelings that we've been trying to escape for much of our lives. To achieve this on a deep level requires that we not use the short-term gratifications of addictions to evade the emotions that we are trying to relate to in therapy.

Most of us have some sort of avoidance techniques. Though some of them are more visible, some are more destructive, and some are more addictive, they all slow our progress in therapy. The compulsive use of alcohol, drugs, food, work, shopping, or television all serve the purpose of helping us to avoid feeling. Working hard in your session won't go very far if afterward you go out and drown your feelings in wine or a shopping binge. This is not to say that you should wait until you've gotten over your addiction to start therapy, but that you may need to focus your work in therapy on the addictive behavior before you're able to go very deeply.

While this book cannot address the huge field of addiction, here are a few key guidelines:

- The relinquishment of some addictions requires medical attention, and others may require specialized treatment.
- Twelve-step programs can be immensely helpful and can work very well in conjunction with psychotherapy.
- At the moment that you consider indulging the addiction, ask yourself:
  - What feeling am I trying to avoid?
  - What might the behavior or substance be a substitute for?

WHAT'S MY THERAPIST GOT TO DO WITH IT?

Why can't I just express myself with my friends and my family? Certainly therapy should not exclude expressing yourself elsewhere, but expressing your feelings in therapy may offer more opportunities for opening channels than elsewhere. Your therapist's focus and neutrality provide a setting to work through feelings that's relatively rare. Your therapist should be empathic, but not distressed about what you're going through. While friends and family may be caring, they may have difficulty being objective, may be too invested in a particular outcome, and may not be able to listen for an extended period of time. Further, many people feel much freer to express themselves in a setting that's completely confidential and where there are no negative consequences for what they say.

As I mentioned earlier in the chapter, a recent study on the emotional impact of crying indicates that crying with one other person seems to have more benefits than crying alone or crying with a group. When we retell a painful story in the presence of an empathic listener, it literally changes the memory of the painful experience so that it doesn't have as much negative impact when it comes up again. This healing process is also being confirmed in neurological studies; we actually create new wiring that makes the memory feel less like an emergency when it arises again. In most cases the presence of another caring person is essential in that change and healing.

Merely retelling a story in a mechanical way won't help; if the remembering isn't accompanied by emotion, the story doesn't really change. In order for the emotion to be accessible, the retelling needs to be done in a safe context. Otherwise the retelling of a painful story may just reinforce your sense that the situation is still dangerous or that you are helpless or powerless.

The original pain and suffering, whether it be sadness, hurt, or disappointment, is bad enough. But a secondary feeling, a reaction to the feeling, such as, *"Oh NO, I'm not going to be able to tolerate feeling this again,"* may make it feel as though something terrible and irreparable is still happening, and can cause additional distress. Retelling the story in the presence of an empathic listener can help you change your experience of that story so that when the memory resurfaces, the secondary feelings don't come with it. When we ruminate on our own, we often rehearse the story in a way that digs a deeper rut. Ideally, with a therapist, the retelling changes the perspective and experience.

Further, when your therapist helps you to contain a feeling without being overwhelmed by it, he or she models a way of handling feelings that you'll internalize over time. Ideally our parents teach us how to self-soothe, but if for some reason they weren't able to do it for you, you'll need to learn how from someone else, so that you can eventually have your feelings rather than your feelings having you.

SUMMARY

1. Open a channel to express your feelings spontaneously, contain them, and get to know them, and then direct the energy from those feelings where it needs to go.
2. It may be helpful at times to put aside certain feelings, suppressing them, once you've dealt with them consciously.
3. Slow down and allow yourself time to get a bodily, felt sense of the emotions that are vague or indistinct.
4. Try to understand the possible message and direction behind emotions, and distinguish them from signals (such as free-floating anxiety) in which the feeling is not to be believed.
5. Use your ego-mayor to make conscious decisions about how to respond to emotions.
6. Don't use addictions to avoid emotions.
7. Allow your therapist to be a healing witness to your emotions.

Chapter Three:

Enough about Them: Look Deeply Within for the Sources of Change

*"Look, call it denial if you like, but I think what goes on in
my personal life is none of my own damn business."*

> *"Yesterday I was clever, so I wanted to change the world. Today I am
> wise, so I am changing myself."*
>
> —Rumi

Three mothers in Florida are talking about their sons in New York
City. The first one says, "See this diamond necklace? My son bought
that for me." The next one says, "Ah, yes, but see that Mercedes-Benz
in the driveway? My son bought that for me." So they turn to the third
mother and ask her what her son has gotten her. She replies: "Ah, my son.
He goes to a Park Avenue psychoanalyst five times a week and pays him

three hundred dollars an hour. And you know what he spends the whole time talking about? Me!"

Part of what it means to "work on it" in therapy is to focus on what we can do to make change rather than focus on things that we can't change—such as other people. We often need to acknowledge and accept aspects of our lives that may be out of our control, and even mourn them, but then we need to move on and focus on what we can control. This includes taking an active role in changing the outer circumstances of our lives, such as who we spend our time with, and where we spend our time. But more importantly it includes looking deep inside for the sources of change that help us to think differently about the outer world and respond differently to it.

There are significant limits to what we can change on the outside, but far fewer limits to how much we can change our inner responses. Using therapy to figure out how to make changes to our environment and circumstances can certainly improve our emotional well-being. But the really powerful changes, the ones that empower us to eventually go out and do the work on our own, are the ones that we make on the inside. Therapy brings about longer-lasting change and empowers us by changing our actual psychology, our attitude and how we respond. Work on our inner life often helps us to eventually make changes on the outside that were not possible before. But perhaps most importantly, focusing within helps us to build an alliance with unconscious resources, directions, and wisdom that are healthy and constructive.

Research indicates that when you have a sense that control comes from within, a sense that you can determine the events of your life, you will benefit more from psychotherapy.[1] Known technically as an internal locus of control (meaning that you locate the control of your life within yourself), this attitude also leads to an overall greater sense of well-being.[2] When we feel that we have more control, we are more likely to take an active role in making better lives for ourselves rather than feeling like passive victims, subject to the whims of the outer world. In Chapter Six we'll talk about how this can backfire if we take too much responsibility, but for now the important thing to keep in mind is that your time in therapy is best spent acknowledging those things that are out of your control, and then looking inside to find the sources of change.

This may seem obvious, but I can tell you from having sat on both sides of the couch, therapy presents a distracting temptation: to focus on the problems outside of us, the situations and people that we imagine are the blocks to our happiness. A certain amount of venting and strategizing about the situation may help, but in the long run, understanding how you got yourself there, why it gets to you so much, and what you get out of it will be some of the most empowering work you do in therapy. You can curse the oil companies for the high price of fuel, but if you operate your car more efficiently you'll have much more control.

The temptation for some in therapy is to spend a lot of their time in session talking about how awful their boss, spouse, parents, children, friends, or enemies are. To some extent this is necessary; again, a certain amount of expressing frustration to someone who cares may release emotional tension and help to change our experience of a difficult situation. And if you are being abused in any way, it's very important that you get help to find a way out of the situation. But, aside from situations of abuse and mistreatment, if we wish to achieve growth that we can take with us when therapy ends, we eventually need to step back and look inside to see if we can learn anything about ourselves from the situation, and what we can do to improve it.

Some people expect that their therapist will "support" them when they are at odds with others. It is helpful for the therapist to validate your *feelings* about the situation, but if the expectation is that the therapist will always validate your *thinking* about the situation, your *interpretation* of it, affirming that you're right and your nemesis is wrong, it will limit what you can get out of the process. It's usually not effective for our therapists to "support" our blind spots. By all means pour out your frustrations; be sure not to skip this step. But also be willing to step back and look at what you might be able to do differently to change the situation, either through communication, different behavior, or by cultivating a different attitude.

I want to be clear that I'm not suggesting that you shut down your feelings about the outside world and the people in it. For instance, if grieving has brought you into therapy, you may need to really sit with the feelings about whom or what you've lost and what you miss about them. This *is* inner work, even though it may appear to be focused on the outside. In a case like this you're not trying to bring something or someone back, you are trying to change the inside by allowing yourself to mourn and come to terms with the loss.

Shakespeare tells us in his play *Hamlet*: "For there is nothing either good or bad, but thinking makes it so." Personally, I think he was exaggerating, but he does have a point.

Psychologist Sonja Lyubomirsky[3] has concluded from her research that our happiness is 50 percent dependent on our genetic set point, only 10 percent on our circumstances, and 40 percent on our intentional thinking and behavior. That 40 percent, our intentional thinking and behavior, is the sweet spot for therapeutic focus and effectiveness, the place where we can make a difference in our lives. If we add to this the emerging evidence that we can even turn genes on or off,[4] we begin to understand that the latitude for control and change may be wider than we had felt before.

Alex

Alex was a tenured professor at a major university where he enjoyed his research and was appreciated by his students. But two other faculty members there were making his life miserable, or so it seemed when he first came to therapy for health issues that his doctors could find no cause for.

His colleagues were in fact formidable: uncooperative, competitive, and just plain unpleasant. And they really were unavoidable. But with a wife who had her own career, and three children well settled in their schools, Alex didn't have the option of leaving town for a position elsewhere. He was reluctant to bring the matter to the appropriate authorities. These two other faculty members were savvy enough to keep their actual behavior within legal margins. The situation seemed hopeless and Alex was at his wit's end.

Alex did get some relief by venting his frustrations. But we both knew that substantial change was going to take more than that.

Our first step was to return some balance to his life. He'd given up exercise and photography years earlier when his children were born. It was time to put those back in place. The exercise improved his brain chemistry with endorphins, and his photography provided a creative outlet and a healthy distraction from obsessing about his colleagues.

But more importantly we had to look at how he thought about his colleagues. I asked him what he imagined about their motivations. His immediate response was that they took pleasure in dominating and in seeing him suffer. I asked him if the situation reminded him of anything, did it feel familiar? It turned out his older brother, Roger, had taken great delight in engaging him in a sort of verbal torture when he was a child, taunting him and humiliating him whenever he could.

Roger (the brother) had been abused physically by their father. As the eldest child, he had been the one to rebel and challenge authority, and he was punished mercilessly for it. Roger handed the abuse down to Alex whenever it seemed Alex was feeling good about himself. Alex learned to keep a low profile and to abandon any appearance of strength in order to stay out of danger.

As we discussed it Alex came to see that his brother had needed desperately to find a way to feel some control and superiority in his life. Unfortunately, he found it at Alex's expense.

This opened a window onto his experience with the other faculty members. He came to see that underneath their bullying demeanor, these were actually frightened children, coping the only way they *knew how in a cutthroat academic environment. It had nothing to do with him, except to the degree that he fell into the defeated attitude and passive position that he had adopted as the younger brother. He realized that the intensity of the emotion he experienced about the situation with his colleagues was amplified with the echoes of his brother's taunting.*

Eventually Alex summoned his own strength and arranged a mediation, which forced his colleagues to curb their most egregious offenses. But more importantly, he separated the past from the present and changed how he viewed the situation: he was not being controlled by his brother, and he was not the victim of his colleagues' insecurities. His dealings with them became more matter-of-fact, not loaded with the history of his brother's abuse. He returned his focus to his original motivation for becoming a professor.

Changing his perspective gave him more of a sense of control, which in turn created a positive feedback loop. Both his mood and his phys-ical health improved. Alex developed a sense of agency in his life, a sense that whatever the external circumstances, he could change both his behavior and his thinking in a way that made the outer situation more livable and the inner one more fulfilling.

So, to get the most out of therapy, you'll want to focus on what goes on inside of you, rather than what's happening outside. This may mean looking at your anger rather than what you feel others are doing wrong, or how you think about germs, rather than the germs themselves, or what you get out of enabling an alcoholic, rather than what a bum he or she is for drinking again.

FIND YOUR BLIND SPOTS

But this business of looking inside isn't always so easy. As you begin to move your attention inward you may start to notice that it's often not so clear what's happening there. You may be able to sense that there are powerful influences that aren't usually in conscious view. We all have blind spots. We all have parts of our psychology that we can't see. What we are able to see, what constitutes our awareness about ourselves, is the proverbial tip of the iceberg,[5,6] the roughly 5 percent that's visible. The other 95 percent of our mind, that unconscious part of ourselves that we're not aware of, has a huge impact on us. This unconscious is the source of both wisdom and the blind spots that can cause trouble in our lives. Becoming more aware of both of these helps to get the different aspects of ourselves working together rather than in opposition.

So, I'm suggesting not only that you keep the main focus on yourself, but also that you direct it *deeply* within yourself, exploring those places that you couldn't see before.

This brings us back to the issue raised at the end of Chapter One, an issue central to the process of psychotherapy: How do I become conscious of something that may be unconscious? Over the last one hundred years, psychotherapy has developed a set of subskills to help us access the unconscious. Like a periscope, these skills help us to see around and through and under, to perceive what was previously out of view. Let's explore some of these.

RECLAIM THE SHADOW PARTS OF YOURSELF THAT YOU'VE PROJECTED ONTO OTHERS

One way to get to know what's happening inside of yourself is to notice what disturbs you about other people. Watch for patterns of the things that lead you to feel critical, angry, or disappointed with others. Whatever it is about them that bugs you may tell you more about yourself than them. You may be projecting onto them things that you don't like about yourself.

Sometimes we prefer to see the parts of our personalities that we have not acknowledged as existing in another person rather than in ourselves. It's as if we're looking in a mirror without being aware of it. We imagine that what we see belongs to someone else, when in fact it belongs to us. The parts of ourselves that we want to deny are known as the shadow. These parts may be aspects of ourselves that we never allow ourselves to live out, or they may be parts that we do live out but deny. And we can project both kinds of shadow onto other people.

If you find yourself talking a lot in session about how controlling and authoritarian your manager is, you may find it helpful to ask yourself whether you allow yourself to claim your own authority and to take control when you need to. Or it may be helpful to ask if you yourself are bossy at times but don't want to admit it. In either case you've tried to disown a part of your shadow, your potential to be a stronger person yourself, and you judge your manager for the behavior you try to repress or deny.

This is not to say that there isn't some truth to your complaints about others. But if you've done everything you can to communicate with the other person about the problem, then it's time to see what you can change within yourself to make the situation better. In this case it would be to consciously use your own authority in a healthy way.

Even if your projection and what you need to own is relatively small, using this tool still puts you in a more active and satisfying position—you're working on it.

Who are the people who really get to you? What do they do that drives you crazy? In some of these situations, if we ask ourselves whether that other person may actually represent something about ourselves that we don't acknowledge, we may come to know ourselves better, and integrate aspects of ourselves that, when conscious, can actually be very helpful. This is known as owning your own shadow.

Projecting either unlived or lived but unacknowledged parts of yourself are both instances of not owning your shadow. The solution is the same in both cases: look within yourself for the things that you criticize others for, and reflect on how you handle those things yourself. Then consciously decide whether the way you handle them is helping or hindering you.

Jim

Jim, a thirty-six-year-old attorney, had been with his girlfriend Rita for about two years when he came into therapy. His presenting problem was that he needed to decide whether to end the relationship. The fact that he had a low-grade depression seemed irrelevant to him.

He loved Rita, but she was beginning to drive him crazy. He had originally loved how free and spontaneous she was, but now that they had moved in together, he had no patience for her sloppiness. She was never on time, she couldn't balance a checkbook, and she left her gym clothes all over the living room.

He would have liked to spend his sessions venting about her. But he knew better.

Jim had learned at an early age to be hyper-responsible. His parents were busy professionals who often left him to take care of his two younger sisters. He got them off to school on time and made sure they kept their things out of the living room so that their parents didn't have a conniption fit. He felt that there wasn't room for error and learned to run a tight ship.

Jim developed a disdain for play and was a serious student by the time he was in the seventh grade. His discipline served him well in succeeding in the outer world. But it had made a disaster of his inner world. He was perpetually in a rush. It didn't matter whether there was a deadline or not. He was known as a slave-driver at work, and he had even been called on the carpet for the way he pressured the people who reported to him.

When we started looking closely at what Rita was actually doing it didn't seem quite as excessive to me as it did to Jim. He seemed to need to paint her in extreme terms: "She's so damn lazy. She watches TV all the time. And she never does any work around the house." According to him they had fallen into a "division of labor"; he did all the work and she did all the play.

It seemed to me that as much as he complained about her, he was getting something out of seeing her as "the lazy one." He even enabled her to be that way to some extent, rolling his eyes, but still picking up after her.

I noted to Jim he would never let himself indulge in the kinds of things she did.

"Damn right," he said.

"Have you ever wanted to?"

"No way."

"Really? Never?"

"Nope. That's just not how I do things."

He said this with great conviction, but I knew that there was more to him than the "I" that was speaking at that moment. I decided to try to reach a different part of him.

"I think it's interesting that you chose someone who is so completely opposite to you." He acknowledged that, and spoke about the utter fascination he had with her the first time he saw her. She was dancing at a party and he couldn't believe that someone could be so loose. Jim didn't dance.

So I asked him, "Did it ever occur to you that you chose her because part of you wants that sort of freedom and playfulness in your life? That it's been a compromise for you to be with her? You get to have the spontaneity you want in your life, but not take responsibility for it. That maybe there's a part of you that wants to be like her, but you attack it by criticizing her?" My questions made him uncomfortable, but he took them in. He didn't like the idea, but this moment was one of his turning points. "Working on it" meant seeing that what he projected onto her actually told us a lot about what he had excluded from his own personality.

Part of Jim's work was to develop a more realistic sense of her, and not see her in such extreme ways: to acknowledge that she wasn't as "lazy" as he liked to make her out. But more importantly, he needed to stop asking her to live out his shadow side, to begin to slow down, and to allow himself to live more freely and spontaneously.

USE YOUR IMAGINATION AND EXPLORE ITS SYMBOLISM

Psychotherapy uses imagination as one way of opening a channel from the unconscious and of removing blind spots. We can use at least two types of imagination: those fantasies that come to us unbidden, either fleeting or persistent, and those that we intentionally create. In both cases, it can be helpful to think less concretely about the fantasies that arise, and to view them more symbolically. As I often tell my students and clients, take it seriously, but don't take it literally. In therapy we usually interpret our imaginings as representations of something going on inside of us, rather than as something that could happen in our outer, concrete world.

A fair amount of what goes on in our heads is fantasy: images that quickly pass across the screen of our mind like five-second commercials, or in lengthy scenarios that are more like soap operas that go on for season after season. While some of these fantasies are practical (they can help us to create and manage a workable and fulfilling outer life), some of them may reveal more about what needs to happen in our inner lives. Sometimes we confuse the two: fantasies that are really about our psychology may be displaced onto our outer world.

So, for instance, if you have persistent thoughts of leaving your job, before you leave, ask yourself whether there is a role or responsibility (other than your actual job) that you've assigned to yourself in life that you don't need to take on anymore. If you're obsessed with getting a larger apartment, first ask yourself what you may need more psychological space for, and how you might be cramping yourself. Before you run to the corner pet store to buy a companion, be curious about what that cute little puppy in the commercial that made you cry may represent inside of you.

In therapy sessions we have an opportunity to engage the imagination in order to access the unconscious. One classic example is the empty chair technique, in which you imagine someone whom you want to talk to is sitting in an empty chair across from you. Let 'em have it. Say whatever you've wanted to say to that person, whether it be anger or love. And THEN, go sit in that chair yourself and speak what you imagine he or she would say back to you. But while this sort of technique can be helpful, we probably use imagination more often in therapy in a less dramatic form, simply conjuring in our mind in a way that gives us access to material inside of us.

For some of you, using imagination may require letting go of an approach that attempts to be direct, rational, and efficient. Being so controlled can be a counterproductive habit, and this may quite possibly be the case for many of you who choose to read a book like this. What may seem like the straightest route may not always be the most effective one. In therapy this means that at times we allow ourselves to flow with imagination rather than always hammering away at specific symptoms. Engaging imagination helps you connect to aspects of your personality that have been left out of your wholeness. Allowing yourself to imagine a worst-case scenario, or what the therapist is thinking of you, or what you'd really like to do rather than being such an upstanding citizen, can all help you to access the unconscious.

CONSIDER THAT YOUR BODY MAY BE EXPRESSING WHAT YOUR WORDS CAN'T

Another important and helpful way to access what's happening deep inside is to consider that the body may be expressing what we are unconscious of. This can manifest in posture or in what we experience as ailments and other physical problems.

Posture can be very revealing; notice if you change it in response to what your therapist says, to what you've said, or to what you're thinking about saying. Do you move back when your therapist makes an interpretation? Are you sitting on the edge of your seat? Do you cross your arms when you're telling her what you did last week? Did you make a fist when you mentioned your brother? Focusing your attention on your body at times can give clues as to what's going on inside. Here again, your time in therapy is an opportunity to observe yourself closely in a way that you don't have opportunity to outside of session.

Developing an awareness of the body may be particularly important for those who have experienced trauma. Some theorists and practitioners believe that the body becomes frozen at the point of trauma, and that any physical action that it needed to take at that time may remain unreleased.[7] Further, trauma short-circuits the thinking circuitry of the brain, and may be best understood via the body, since words may not be available.[8]

While it's important to take all illness seriously, it's helpful to consider that some of our physical complaints may have a more psychological origin. This is not to say that it's all in your head, it just may mean that it started in the back of your head and went to your body when it couldn't find a more direct route into consciousness. It could mean that your body is trying to express something your conscious mind hasn't let in yet. The physical symptom and the suffering are real, but the source of them may be emotional. Becoming aware of what the body is expressing may help the symptom to remit.

The "message" may be as vague as, "All this pressure is killing me," or something more specific, as with a conversion disorder, in which the psychological problem is converted to a physical problem. Conversion disorders *appear* to indicate neurological problems that affect muscular systems and sense functions, when in fact there is no real neurological problem. So, for instance, your leg could become paralyzed if you're conflicted about moving forward, or you could become deaf if there is something you don't want to hear.

It's always best to have medical clearance of a problem before considering that the issue may be emotional. The symptoms of illnesses such as hyperthyroidism, anemia, Lyme disease, and most ulcers may appear at first to be the result of emotional issues, but must be treated with appropriate medical interventions.

Still, approximately 60 percent of visits to doctor's offices reveal no diagnosable condition. It's not unusual for emotional problems to either be confused with medical ones, or to actually cause medical ones. Feeling run-down is a common side effect of depression. Anxiety certainly contributes to irritable bowel syndrome. It's best not to jump to a conclusion that any illness is psychological in origin, but many clients have had realizations about themselves by being curious about the meaning of their physical symptoms. This way of thinking, being curious about what the body might be expressing, is one example of a less literal and more symbolic way of understanding ourselves. And it helps to access the unconscious blind spots.

WHAT DO YOU GET OUT OF IT? EXPLORE THE POSSIBILITIES OF UNCONSCIOUS MOTIVATION

Blind spots can leave us unaware of certain motivations and their powerful influence. Many of our basic motivations, including security, autonomy, power, love, productivity, and sensual gratification, develop when we we're quite young, usually before we're conscious, and they don't always develop in a balanced, healthy way. Becoming conscious of these motivations, and the conflicts between them, is part of what makes psychotherapy effective.

Our behavior is not random. It has purpose and meaning, even when what we're doing makes no sense to us. In therapy we consider that we have motivations that we have not become aware of yet, unconscious motivations that cause the behavior that brought us to therapy. "Working on it" in therapy means really questioning why we engage in self-destructive behavior and what we get out of it so that we can make more conscious decisions about our behavior in the future.

While it's usually not obvious at first, there may be some gratification to dysfunctional behavior and attitudes; there may be something that actually feels good underneath the self-defeating things we do. No matter how much your conscious ego says it doesn't like the problem, another little part of you inside may get something out of it. Here are some ways that this may show up:

- If you've gotten the impression that suffering is virtuous, you may invite and engage in suffering. It may feel gratifying to prove that someone has been mean to you, that once again you've been wronged, and that therefore (in a skewed logic), you are a good person.
- We may be inclined to rev up our anger if it makes us feel strong, or if we are trying to prove that we are better than another person.
- It may feel gratifying to focus on negative things so that we can prove that trying is futile. It gets us off the hook.
- If we keep choosing disappointing partners, it may have the gratification of proving that we've been let down and will always be let down.

Don't assume that you're too rational for any of these dynamics. In fact, if you do pride yourself on being a reasonable person, you may be more vulnerable to not-so-reasonable rebellions from within.

When you can recognize these sorts of motivations and feel their gratifications, see your investment in them and acknowledge them, you open up the possibility for more conscious behavior and make progress. Once you have a realization of this sort it will take time to work it through so that you don't have to respond in the same way. It will also be important to find other gratifications that are more fulfilling.

Here's a brief example of what I mean by looking deeply within, past blind spots, to understand motivation. If someone has hurt you, it will feel much worse if you interpret his or her action as deliberately intended to hurt you, that is, to take it personally. But if you consider that perhaps the other person isn't well, or isn't capable of being more considerate, you may suffer less. Taking a different perspective may well be more accurate and less painful.

So this is a reasonable, simple, and fairly effective technique: question your interpretation of a situation in order to give you greater control over your state of mind. But chances are that you may need to take this further; why would you want to assume that person wants to hurt you? What is the gratification in seeing the situation that way? Do you need for some old wounding to be witnessed? Or does it make you feel better about yourself by comparing yourself? Again, looking at your motivations may help you to understand your inner workings in a way that will have payoffs far beyond the specific situation.

It's very important that you not blame or judge yourself for any unconscious motivations you discover. We all have them. The real question is how much we can acknowledge these motivations, and whether we find the right place for that energy to flow. We will discuss this more in Chapter Six, but for now be aware that self-criticism can block the process of becoming aware of your blind spots and unconscious motivations.

ALLY YOURSELF WITH THE GOALS OF THE CONSTRUCTIVE UNCONSCIOUS

While you may find some of your unconscious motivations embarrassing at first, it's important to recognize that they may actually have something far more purposive and constructive at their core. If we look at deeper levels of these motivations, we may see that they have a healthier drive underlying them that has gone awry, and that the unhealthy gratification was only a substitute for the more fulfilling purpose that was blocked.

Sometimes psychological problems are an indication that we're unconsciously trying to work out a problem or expand our personality. There is a part of you, which I call the constructive unconscious, whose natural inclination is to move toward wholeness, toward a personality that's healthy and balanced and can adjust to a wide variety of circumstances. This constructive unconscious has the capacity for self-healing, problem solving, creativity, and expanding the personality to make it more adaptive—if we don't get in its way.

Looking on the inside not only helps us to be aware of "negative" aspects of our personalities, it also leads to an awareness of an inner compass, a center that we can use for direction. The unconscious has been seen by some as a collection of repressed memories. But if you look more closely, you can see that there are also deeper levels of the unconscious that can serve as a source of wisdom, healing, and personal evolution. When we understand our relationships, fantasies, motivations, and dreams at a deep enough level we begin to see an internal motivation toward growth and wholeness. When the hero or heroine goes into the wilderness and slays the dragons of immaturity, overprotection, fear, greed, resentment, or regret, there's usually a treasure there too that he or she can claim. That treasure is a working connection with the constructive unconscious.

Like the conscious ego, the constructive unconscious operates from intent. This intent has been described with such terms as self-regulation, balance, and homeostasis. While these descriptions are partially accurate, I don't think that they convey everything that's happening beneath the surface: the constructive unconscious intends not just survival, but also personal evolution, a personality rich with different facets that help us to thrive in a variety of circumstances.

We're goal-driven creatures. The goals of the unconscious arise primarily from instinct, but these instincts go far beyond food, sex, and shelter. Our original goal was to simply survive and pass on our own genes, but over time we've developed additional goals, far more varied and nuanced, that broaden our range of adaptability. We have evolved instincts to fulfill not only basic biological and security needs, but also more complex psychological needs such as attachment, exploration, play, spirituality, healing, and mastery.

Whether consciousness cooperates or not, the unconscious will pursue these goals. These goals are part of what make us human and healthy. Reaching them leads to wholeness and a sense of fulfillment. In many ways the unconscious is far more wise than consciousness; it often knows better what we need than consciousness does.

Current research provides support for this idea. We now have studies that demonstrate that unconscious thought has a number of advantages over conscious thought in making complex decisions, problem solving, and creativity: it can consider more than seven items at once, it can include information that would have been excluded by consciousness, it can avoid the rules and rigid biases that typically limit consciousness, and it's better than conscious thought at assigning value in decisions.[9]

But the unconscious is effective not only in processing the complex decisions that consciousness presents to it; it's also effective in pursuing goals even when we're not aware of it doing so. Consider the work of Yale psychologist John Bargh, whose research demonstrates how easily the unconscious may be primed to pursue a goal, and to then significantly drive our behavior to reach that goal—all without our knowing.[10]

In their research, Bargh and his colleagues read or mention specific key words or phrases (for instance, "do your best to achieve" or "cooperate") during the first stage of the experiment without the subject being aware of their significance. In doing so they surreptitiously plant ideas in their subjects' unconscious minds that "prime" or predispose them to certain goals. When the subject gets to the actual experiment, the researchers measure the degree to which the primed goal affects the behavior of the subjects. The results are quite remarkable; those subjects who were primed did try harder to cooperate and achieve, and they had neither awareness of the "primed" goal nor any sense of how it altered their behavior.

If psychologists can do this by priming a subject by planting a few words into his or her unconscious, how much more powerful might the intrinsic intent toward psychological adaptivity and wholeness be after being primed by nature for hundreds of thousands of years?

But here's the catch: while our unconscious drive toward psychological health usually proceeds organically and unnoticed as we mature, this natural inclination may be blocked, exaggerated, skewed, or hijacked, leading to a distortion of that natural tendency, and causing psychological and physical problems. Then the constructive unconscious needs assistance from consciousness to get back on track.

Let's look at the same list that I gave earlier in this chapter from a deeper perspective:

- So for instance, if you do get some gratification out of suffering, it may be an indication that you're trying to feel good about yourself, to heal wounds to your self-esteem, but you don't know a better way yet.
- Anger may also mean that you are gathering energy to appropriately protect yourself, but the threat may be long gone and you're fighting an old battle.
- The giving up that comes with depression may be the only way you know how to slow down, look inside, and let go of a way of living that takes far too much responsibility. It is an unconscious effort not to care to such an unhealthy degree.
- Choosing partners who end up being a bad fit may be an unconscious effort to connect with personality traits that you haven't integrated yourself. You may also be unconsciously trying to master and work through a painful relationship from your past.

Looking inside to understand what we are trying to work out is often more effective than seeing problems simply as the result of a bad childhood. Therapy can then help us recognize these deeper motivations and work with them.

As we'll explore in Chapter Ten, the blockage of this natural tendency serves as a signal to look within and an opportunity to ally ourselves with the resources we all carry within us.

SUMMARY

1. Vent your frustrations, but then explore why you react as you do.
2. Use your imagination to explore your inner world.
3. Reclaim the shadow that you have projected onto others— the good and the bad.
4. Ask what your body may be expressing.
5. Explore your motivations and investments: What do you get out of living this way?
6. Look for the original adaptive intent from your constructive unconscious that has been blocked by overprotective strategies.

Chapter Four:

Don't Hold Back: Forge an Authentic Connection with Your Therapist

"I'm thinking 'woof-woof' but I'm saying 'arf-arf.'"

"In my early professional years I was asking the question: How can I treat, or cure, or change this person? Now I would phrase the question in this way: How can I provide a relationship which this person may use for his own personal growth?"

—Carl R. Rogers

Interactions with your therapist offer a rare opportunity to practice the tools from the first three chapters: authenticity, emotional expression, and looking deeply inside. Being direct and openly discussing your personal experience of him or her helps you to take off the mask and develop the capacity for a more authentic relationship, and to involve diverse parts of your personality. Expressing your reactions to him or her presents a chance to have emotions without the emotions having you. And because we often project our own thoughts and feelings onto the therapist, exploring what you imagine your therapist is thinking or feeling can eventually lead to greater knowledge about what's happening inside of you.

Exercising these three tools with your therapist also helps to promote perhaps the most indispensable of all the aspects of psychotherapy: the therapeutic relationship. If you prefer, you can call it the therapeutic alliance, because I know that for some of you, calling your relationship with your therapist, well, a relationship might make you uncomfortable.

While many of you may welcome a strong connection with your therapist, others among you may be cautious. For what it's worth, lots of coolheaded research scientists have come to the same conclusion: the quality of your connection with your therapist is a major factor in the effectiveness of your work in psychotherapy.[1] But it takes two to tango. Your therapist can't create this without you.[2]

For those who may be saying, "Spare me the relationship. Let's get on with the work," I get it. Some of us need more space than others, and therapy needs to account for that. But there's space, and then there's s-p-a-c-e that's so distancing the work can't really come together. And getting on with the work is all packaged up with that alliance.

THE KING'S SPEECH

The King's Speech, a 2010 film based on actual history, serves as an example of the importance of being direct and of letting your therapist into your life as someone personally important.

It's 1925 and Prince Albert, the Duke of York, has a serious problem. As British royalty, and, after his brother, next in line to the throne of England, it's incumbent upon him to address his subjects both publically and via the "wireless" (which at the time meant the radio). But a chronic and pervasive stammer has left him humiliated and his audiences painfully disappointed whenever he speaks. After numerous attempts to solve the problem with traditional speech therapists have failed, he tries working with Lionel Logue.

Logue is an Australian with plenty of experience and no credentials. But he's no pushover. He requires equality in their work—a first-name basis both ways. Success, he asserts, requires an authentic relationship. The duke would prefer to keep it "strictly business, no personal nonsense." But Lionel insists and is willing to risk losing the most prestigious client of his career. He also insists on getting to the root of the problem, rather than working on superficial mechanics. Faced with a seemingly impossible task, and Lionel's proof that the duke can in fact speak perfectly well under the right circumstances, the duke—now Bertie—signs on to the program.

Though he's a decorated naval commander, Bertie finds this far more challenging than anything he's encountered before. He's forced to let down his regal persona in front of a commoner for the definitively undignified exercises that are required: rolling on the floor, head shaking, jaw dropping, and tongue wagging. These appear to be mechanical exercises designed to loosen the tongue, the throat, and the jaw.

But it's not hard to see that doing these in the presence of Lionel also loosens the personality of someone who's been boxed in his entire life. Lionel gets him to sing what he can't say. The duke steps out of his comfort zone, curses, and, more importantly, allows himself to directly express his anger at Lionel. Interestingly, he has no problem speaking when he lets his fury rip. In short, even though this all provides material that would have made a perfectly scandalous and viral YouTube video, he invests in the therapy, and in Lionel himself.

As the work progresses it gets personal. Bertie begins to allow Lionel to see beneath the royal façade and into the sources of his stammer: being forced to function right-handedly even though he's a lefty, being pressured by his father to just get over the stammer, and being humiliated about it by his brother. Lionel comes to see that Bertie is scared, "afraid of his own shadow." He suggests that Bertie may fear his own aspirations to ascend the throne rather than his brother, who is first in line, but clearly not equipped for the position.

Their relationship has its ups and downs but progresses to the point that when the brother abdicates and Bertie is to become king, he wants Lionel there for the coronation: "I should like for the doctor to be seated in the king's box." The archbishop is aghast at the possibility, but Bertie insists. At this point the archbishop does some digging and reveals that Lionel is not in fact a doctor as Bertie had assumed. Bertie confronts Lionel, questions his credentials, and accuses him of fraud and letting the English people down just before the coronation and the war to come. Lionel clarifies that he never misrepresented himself, and that through years of experience he came to realize that his job was to give his clients faith in their own voice by listening to them. At the end of an intense and very personal argument Bertie shouts at Lionel, "I have a voice!"—a proclamation far more effective than any lesson in mechanics would ever be.

The film builds to the moment when Bertie, as newly crowned King George VI, is to give a radio address at the outset of the Second World War. Lionel is there and supports the king through the challenge: "Forget everything else and just say it to me as a friend." The king has found his voice and the speech is a success.

While therapists don't become friends with their clients, when the work goes well, they've usually been allowed some place of importance in their life—just as Lionel was given a place in the king's box at the coronation. Many clients come to therapy hoping just to work out the mechanics, keeping distance from their therapist, not unlike the king in this film. But as King George found out, it's really the relationship that heals.

USING THE THERAPEUTIC ALLIANCE

There are two principal ways that your alliance with your therapist helps you to change: The first is insight. You discover things about how you relate to others and yourself by exploring how you relate to your therapist. The second is at least as powerful but more subtle and difficult to observe. We refer to this as the corrective emotional experience. What you experience with your therapist ideally heals old wounds. But this takes more than showing up. It takes opening up.

I'll explain these more, but first allow me to explore, just as examples, some of the reasons that some of you may be reluctant to even say "therapeutic relationship," and then I'll go on to explain why it's not a good idea to bypass it.

Some people feel uncomfortable with the idea of relying on a therapist for help, and so they try to maintain what they believe is an appropriate and professional distance from their therapist. I admire the determination to be self-sufficient, but I also know that our brains seem to be wired to change through human connection.[3] Just how close that connection needs to become varies somewhat. For some, learning to depend on their therapist is a necessary part of their healing, and for others too much dependence is contraindicated. But I think that for many the really important thing is not so much the degree of dependence, it's allowing the therapist to be a real and significant person in your life.

The dependency that sometimes develops in therapy resolves with time and actually increases the capacity for independence.[4] Therapy ideally prepares us to continue our psychological work on our own when we're ready to stop meeting with our therapist. However, trying to avoid *feelings* of dependency, attachment, or closeness so that the therapist isn't too important to us may limit what we can get out of therapy. And relegating the therapist to a safe distance may further deepen patterns of detachment. It could also lengthen your course of therapy rather than shorten it.

For others the greater challenge is to be direct and authentic with their therapist. Ideally the foundation of your relationship with your therapist is characterized by rapport, basic positive regard, on both sides. But you may well also have many other feelings about him or her that come and go, and you may well have lots of reactions, both negative and positive, to what he or she does or doesn't do as part of your work together. The more you can be open to your feelings in the therapeutic setting, and the more you can discuss what goes on between the two of you, the more effective your work will be.[5] Not speaking your piece prevents the sort of interactions that make the process come alive and fuel its effectiveness. And holding back may be just another way of maintaining distance.

But many clients are afraid to express any feelings about their therapist, particularly negative ones. While there are many reasons that could account for this, for some people it mirrors a theme in their outer life: a fear of biting the hand that feeds them emotionally. If someone feels important to us, if that person's emotional support helps to sustain us, we may feel that we have to be careful around that person and not say anything that could upset him or her.

This feeling often occurs in therapy, and that's a good thing because it gives you an opportunity to experiment. Tell your therapist what you're going through and see what happens. The experience of processing your feelings with your therapist can be both illuminating and healing. If doing so seems difficult, just start by telling your therapist that it's hard to be direct with her. That in itself would be a very effective piece of work.

A final example of the kind of issues that people run into in forging the therapeutic alliance is that some people are puzzled by it; they find it hard to believe that it's both professional and personal at the same time. Good therapists set good practical boundaries, but they also allow themselves to genuinely care about the people they are working with. If you find this hard to believe, your feelings about the arrangement may also inform you as to how you relate to people in general. Again, talk about it.

To explore how this all actually plays out in psychotherapy, I'll discuss the role relationship plays in human psychological growth in general and in psychotherapy in particular. Then I'll discuss how the first three tools are used in regard to your psychotherapist. Finally I'll discuss some specific areas of communication with your therapist, all of which contribute to both insight and corrective emotional experience.

THE THERAPEUTIC ALLIANCE FACILITATES ADAPTATION AND GROWTH

The human brain is a social brain; it has evolved to grow and adapt through its connections to others.[6] Individual neurons in the brain function just as individual people do; the better their connection with other neurons, the more flexible and adaptive they are. Without these connections, neurons "feel" totally useless and die off in a process called apoptosis.

Similarly, the better the quality of our connections with others, the better we are able to change and grow. And just like those disconnected and depressed neurons in the brain, when we're disconnected from others, we may feel our lives are meaningless and we kill ourselves off, figuratively, with depression, or even literally.[7] Institutionalized infants who are not held, who don't develop connections with others, often die from that lack of connection.[8] Your connection with your therapist is in itself healing, but should also help open the way for better connections with others.

Recent studies[9] that wed brain research with clinical research to further understand how therapy helps, confirm the centrality of the therapeutic alliance in healing and growth. The results verify that the circulation of ideas and feelings between therapist and client constitute a significant part of what actually alters the brain. We are wired to change through interpersonal connection.

The therapeutic setting also serves as a microcosm of your life that fosters insight: the way that you relate there and the experiences that you have there often mirror what happens in your larger world. Exploring these patterns in therapy can be quite valuable in understanding and changing yourself. It allows you to see more clearly what you do and don't do that works for you or against you, and gives you a place to actually exercise that insight in a way that leads to change.

Therapy creates a unique and safe environment that allows us to slow down and pay close attention to ourselves in a very detailed way so that we can live more consciously in our everyday lives. It's a bit like playing a video in slow motion so that we can observe our thinking, feeling, and behavior more clearly. We can see and learn from what is usually passed over in everyday life. When you can explore the emotions you're having in the moment you're having them, you have the greatest opportunity to change.

As I wrote in Chapter Two, when you speak about disturbing emotional issues in the presence of someone you feel you can trust and who you feel cares about you, the disturbing experience is coded differently in the brain and becomes less disturbing. This can also happen when you process issues that come up with your therapist. Any issues that arise between you and your therapist may feel related to previous hurtful experiences, and working them through with your therapist can impact the older historical issues that are similar. When you experience them in session with your therapist it's real— not just theoretical or at a safe distance—and the emotions and ideas are more malleable, more open to influence and reworking. This is known as a corrective emotional experience.

COMMUNICATION PROVIDES PRACTICE IN TAKING OFF THE MASK AND BEING AUTHENTIC

Many clients feel uncomfortable being direct; they fear that they'll reveal parts of themselves they'd rather hide. Therapy offers an opportunity to experiment with exposing these parts of yourself so that you can eventually integrate them into your personality in a healthy way. This could mean disagreeing with an interpretation that your therapist makes, expressing anger at her for running late or cancelling, telling her that you feel she isn't challenging you enough, or acknowledging that she's been helpful and that you like her. Whatever part of you that you've been reluctant to show, therapy offers an opportunity for that voice to be heard and included.

Some of you, however, may feel so comfortable being direct that it's even gotten you in trouble, and that's actually one of your problems. This is good to acknowledge. But still, don't hold back. Therapy is a good place to bring it on. Give your therapist a real taste of what you're like in the outside world and then step back and look at it. There may be good reasons for your communication style that, once understood, will help you to be more effective at getting what you want or advocating for what you believe.

As an example, some people feel that it's important to confront authority, and their therapist may feel like an authority to them. If this is your style, the work might entail understanding your need to challenge authority and finding more effective ways to do it. Those with this tendency to challenge have an important role in the community: speaking out about what isn't working and what isn't fair. But fulfilling that role effectively may require polishing their skills of confrontation so that the message can shine through. This isn't just about resolving a conflict with an oppressive father, though it's possible that would need to be clarified and worked through. It may more importantly be about becoming skillful in challenging the way things are so that you can honor your gifts and calling. The key action is to engage that part of you with your therapist in a genuine way, not just discuss it theoretically.

COMMUNICATION PROVIDES PRACTICE IN EXPRESSING A FEELING AND THEN OBSERVING IT

Communicating with your therapist is another place where an alternating rhythm of jumping into feeling and then standing back and observing can be effective. Don't be afraid to voice your thoughts and feelings about your therapist; you might be exactly right, and your therapist will probably be happy to get feedback. But also be willing to step back, let go of your preconceptions, and be curious about what you're feeling and thinking.

To be very simplistic about it (as the brain is actually far more complex), when you express your feelings about your therapist spontaneously you operate first out of your right brain (which is more holistic, intuitive, and emotional), and then when you reflect on what is going on underneath you switch to your left brain (which is more analytical, verbal, logical, and orderly). Going back and forth between the two expands the corpus callosum, the band of fibers that unites the two hemispheres and helps them to work together.

Speaking openly with your therapist may be one aspect of therapy that creates the states of moderate arousal that lead to learning. If the anxiety is too intense, it's hard to learn, but if it's too low, you have less motivation to change.

Communicating with your therapist about your experience of him or her is one way to open up the emotional dimmer switch that I referred to in Chapter Two. Notice the uncomfortable feelings about your therapist as they start to rise up the pipeline, and give voice to them rather than cutting them off, or acting them out. The feelings may seem subtle and quiet at first, but with communication they become more audible.

What about Sexual Feelings?

One of the advantages of the therapeutic relationship is that anything you feel or say is acceptable. This includes sexual feelings. You should feel free to discuss any sexual feelings you have toward your therapist without fear that it would result in any actual sexual behavior. But while *discussion* of sexual feelings is invited, *acting* on them would be very destructive. To be perfectly clear: a healing therapeutic relationship does not include sexual activity. Any psychotherapist who has sex with his or her client is abusing them. It's that simple.

FEELINGS AND IDEAS ABOUT YOUR THERAPIST PROVIDE ACCESS TO YOUR UNCONSCIOUS

In Chapter Three I described how we may project unwanted parts of ourselves onto other people. Hopefully you'll do this with your therapist. What you imagine about your therapist, and what you imagine your therapist is thinking about you, may give you some pretty good clues as to what's actually going on inside of you, clues about what you think of yourself and what you might think of others. This isn't to say that everything you think or imagine about your therapist is just a fabrication. You may be entirely accurate, but this still may inform us as to what goes on inside of you.

Sometimes we unconsciously assume that others, including our therapist, think the same way we do. For instance, if we tend to be self-critical, we may imagine that our therapist is critical of us. On the other hand, sometimes we attribute to our therapist things that we haven't consciously owned, shadow aspects that we'd rather deny. If you haven't acknowledged your own vulnerability, you may imagine that the therapist is afraid of losing you as a patient, because he is afraid of losing income or of losing face if you leave the treatment. This could be a reflection of your own fears rather than those of your therapist.

Here is an example of a client using all three of the tools from the first three chapters—authenticity, channeling feeling, and looking within—all directly with the therapist.

Ralph

Ralph was a fifty-nine-year-old father of three and entrepreneur who came to therapy because he was so consumed by work and so controlling that his wife and kids had virtually given up on having a real relationship with him. His wife was ready for a divorce.

Ralph was a hard worker, to put it mildly. It would be more accurate to say that he was both obsessive and compulsive about work. He wouldn't—rather couldn't—stop himself from thinking about work and doing everything possible to make his business a bigger success. When it was too late to contact possible clients by phone or in person, he was scouring the Internet for ways to boost business.

This way of approaching life showed up in therapy too. He was determined to hold onto his family, and tried hard to figure out what to do. He used a very intellectualized approach, quoting philosophers he had read in college years ago. At first I tried to meet him and work with him in his more cerebral way, but the results were limited.

So on one occasion I let myself silently and intuitively try to imagine what it felt like to be Ralph. This actually wasn't so easy to do, but he didn't see it that way. He became impatient and frustrated when I didn't respond immediately to everything he said. I asked him what he imagined was going on. He was reluctant at first, but was eventually able to tell me that he imagined that I was just coasting and that I must be thinking about my upcoming vacation. He imagined that I had stayed up late last night watching travel videos and was too tired to really focus on his issues.

Now it's true that I enjoy planning and taking vacations, but fatigue wasn't what was causing the situation between us at that moment. It turned out that Ralph hadn't taken a vacation in years—he said he didn't need one—and he believed that people who did take vacations were really weak or not invested in their work. He projected onto me what he had not allowed in himself.

As is often the case when people are engaged closely in work together, Ralph had picked up that something different was going on with me, but he didn't correctly interpret just what that was. He was right in that I was taking a vacation from the more cerebral way we had been trying to work; I was using imagination and intuition rather than directed thinking. But he added to that bit of truth the idea that I was indulging in leisure, something he had never allowed himself, and so tended to project onto others.

Ralph and I were both using imagination about what was happening between us now, and it allowed us to break through a standstill. When we use this sort of imagination in therapy we may be accessing either experiences from the past that are not worked through, or issues that are going on inside of us right now. It is not unusual for both to be true.

In Ralph's case he experienced my reverie about him, my use of imagination rather than constant talking, as an abandonment. This felt similar to the way his parents had abandoned him when they were too distracted to pay attention to him. As a bootstraps sort of guy, Ralph wanted to deny that what his parents had done or not done forty-five years ago could possibly make a difference in how he lived now. He felt that what happened in his life was all his responsibility. So instead of dealing consciously with the disappointment of his parents being unavailable, he transferred the abandonment he had experienced with his parents to me, seeing me as the one who abandoned him.

At the same time he projected an aspect of himself that he had never owned, the ability to let go and take a vacation from his regimented way of life. In effect he was right that he was responsible for the problems in his life; he had been abandoning significant aspects of himself in order to propel his business forward.

We revisited this interaction many times in our subsequent work, and while it took time for him to own his own emotional needs, he eventually was able to integrate them into a more balanced lifestyle for himself.

In this example Ralph exhibited what I have referred to earlier as a sort of rhythm in the work. He was able to engage his imagination, say *what he thought and felt without reservation, and then step back and look at what might be going on inside of him.*

What was at least as important for Ralph in this session—and this is what caused his original hesitancy to tell me what he felt—was that he hadn't wanted to admit to either of us that my presence and involvement in the work was important to him. He had felt that he should be able to do it all on his own. Just acknowledging this and allowing a working alliance between us helped him to widen his personality: he didn't stop working hard, but he did start to make room for others in his life.

REENACTING, REMEMBERING, AND REWORKING

My experience with Ralph demonstrates one reason why many therapists are somewhat reserved about what they share about their personal lives: if you know too much about your therapist, there's less that you can project onto him or her, and less opportunity to learn about yourself.

This example also sheds some light on why therapists explore the past. While there are variations among therapists about this, many of us believe that the problem is not so much what happened in our past as it is that we are living as if it were *still* the past. As George Santayana famously said, "Those who cannot remember the past are condemned to repeat it."[10] Elucidating the past is just one way of pulling back the curtain and revealing some of our motivations for the way we negotiate life in the present.

And here is one of the many places where your relationship with your therapist proves useful; we often unwittingly replicate early parental relationships with our therapist. Through an unconscious process of reenacting, we remember and recreate old situations, and in doing so create an opportunity to rework old adaptations that have not served us well.[11]

Some of this remembering is accessed through imagination: what we imagine about our therapist may indicate more about our early life than the present (for instance, your therapist really isn't going to criticize you as your mother did—it just feels that way). And believe it or not, this is a good thing because it presents an opportunity to actually experience and become aware of the way you have tried to adjust in life, and an opportunity to find a new way to do it. Without the actual experience, it may be just an intellectual exercise that doesn't really change you much. But if you can bring the experience to consciousness and talk about it, you can find a better way of dealing with it.

Much of how we live our lives is based upon implicit memory, that is, memory that is stored unconsciously, but still affects our moment-to-moment decisions and behavior. In order to access these implicit memories, we need a situation where these memories can be reexperienced, and where we can observe our responses carefully. In effect, by exploring what happens with our therapist, we're doing our own research about the impact that implicit memory has on how we perceive and relate to others. Voicing our experience of the therapist gives us important information about how implicit memory creates our default patterns.

Again, none of this is to say that what you experience with your therapist isn't in some way real, but it is to say that it may have far more meaning than is apparent at first.

COMMUNICATION WILL HELP YOUR THERAPIST HELP YOU

Therapy ideally proceeds as a collaboration and partnership. Your therapist's interpretations—her hypotheses as to what is going on inside of you—won't always be *just* right. But if you can, take her idea, and, just as a jazz musician might, improvise on her theme. In what way might it be accurate? Take what he or she says and see how the two of you together can improve on the original idea so that it resonates more, developing an insight that feels more true to your experience. Collaboration requires communication, from both parties, about their experience in the sessions. It's not magic.

One of the patterns I have often seen when I work with couples is that one or both of the partners believe that *if* their partner really cared about them and loved them, he or she would be able to intuit what they need without them having to ask for it. They feel that if they ask for what they need it's meaningless once they get it since it wasn't offered freely. So, in order to protect themselves from being vulnerable and hurt, they may never ask anyone to respond to their needs, fearing that they would be humiliated if they did hope to be cared about.

I suggest that you not expect your therapist or anyone else to read your mind, no matter how long you've been with that person. I've worked with couples who had been together for thirty years who realized in therapy that they were mistaken in what they believed the other person thought and felt.

Therapists can't always intuit all of your needs, try as we may. And it doesn't necessarily mean that your therapist isn't engaged in the work with you if she can't intuit your needs. In fact, if your therapist never failed to understand you, and never made a mistake, you'd be missing an opportunity. Through various unintentional minor mistakes, therapists disappoint their clients' idealizations and expectations, and in doing so create the mild to moderate stress that helps the client to grow—*if* the client sticks it out and works it through consciously.[12] I don't know any therapists who would intentionally make a mistake to disappoint their client to achieve this. But I do know hundreds of therapists who are quite human and perfectly imperfect.

Idealizing your therapist, believing, for example, that he or she could intuit all of your feelings and needs, may have its benefits early on in the process. But if it goes on too long, you might consider exploring whether that serves an unconscious purpose for you.

I remember when I was completing my analytic training and finishing work with one of my supervisors. I told her that I had never felt judged by her. I imagined that she was a meditator and had done a lot of work through her meditation that allowed her to be non-judgmental. She said, "No, it's nothing like that. It's just that I know that I have my own crap." She helped to dismantle my idealization and replace it with a picture of a very human being, which was a much more helpful vision for me as I went on to work independently.

One day a young student at a Buddhist monastery goes to meditate with two experienced monks as part of his education. They walk around to the opposite side of the lake from the monastery and are about to start their morning meditation when the first monk realizes he has forgotten his mat. So he walks up to the lake and walks calmly across the surface of the water to the monastery and returns with his mat. Suddenly the second monk realizes that he's forgotten his sun hat. So he runs across the surface of the water to the monastery and returns with a straw hat. The student is astounded by this and at the end of the meditation he tries to walk across the water. He falls straight in and emerges soaking wet. The two monks look on and after watching his failed attempts for a while the first monk says to the second, "Do you think we should tell him where the stones are?"

Your therapist, like the monks, might not be as superhuman as she seems at first, and recognizing this can be an important step toward finding your own inner resources. Don't feel that you need to go along silently with how the therapist manages the sessions or handles the relationship. Ask about what's going on, and, as much as possible, bring your curiosity and feelings into the room. Letting her know what you're going through in the process is valuable information that can help her to help you.

This is not to say that expressing what you think you need will always lead the therapist to choose to fulfill that need. Exploring the desire, analyzing it, and understanding what it means may be more helpful than satisfying it. That may really be the best way for your therapist to honor the deeper needs that you have for self-understanding and growth.

TAKIN' CARE OF BUSINESS

There's no getting around it; your therapist makes his or her living doing this. That means that either he or she, or the clinic where you see your therapist, needs to get paid. Whether you are using insurance or paying out of pocket, payment of the fee may become an opportunity for fruitful discussion.

Are you supposed to pay for that session that you forgot about? What about that session you missed because you got caught in that once-every-hundred-years traffic jam? What happens when your insurance runs out? If you lose your job, what would it mean if your therapist did or did not lower your fee?

Ideally the two of you sorted these things out in the initial consultation; therapists have different approaches to the practical boundaries that we call "the frame," and it's best to know these up front. But it's quite likely that some gray area will come up that the two of you could not have foreseen. This is a good thing. It's real, and it's an opportunity to be direct and to explore how you interact with others.

The way to use these situations is to explore what they mean to you and what you imagine they mean to your therapist: What if she does charge you? What if she doesn't? What does it mean that you're six weeks behind in your payment? How do you think your therapist feels about it? Bring in the part of you that wants her to let you do whatever you want. Bring in the part of you that resents having to pay her to just sit there and listen to you. Let yourself feel whatever it is you feel, talk about it, and then reflect on it. Don't dismiss these possibilities too quickly; they could pay off in understanding yourself and learning about how you deal with people.

COMMUNICATION PREVENTS PREMATURE TERMINATION

An aspiring monk wanted to find a spiritual teacher. He goes to a monastery and the teacher tells him, "You can stay here but we have one important rule: all students observe the vow of silence. You will be allowed to speak once after every twelve years." So the young monk practices silently and diligently for twelve long years, and the day comes when he can make one statement or ask one question. So he says, "The bed is too hard." He keeps going for another twelve years of hard, silent meditation and gets the opportunity to speak again. He says, "The food tastes bad." Twelve more years of hard work and he gets to speak again. After thirty-six years of practice he finally says, "I quit." His teacher quickly answers, "Good, all you've been doing is complaining anyway."

When we don't have the freedom to communicate openly a glut of feelings can build up and erode relationship. Resentment is just one of many feelings that can make us want to leave. Any relationship in which people don't feel safe expressing themselves or advocating for themselves is doomed to a short and miserable life. It's the same in therapy.

Perhaps the most unfortunate mistake I see people making in their therapy is not speaking to their therapist about their discontent, and then leaving without having a chance to see what might be learned. There are many reasons that clients leave prematurely; some of them are conscious and some of them aren't. The client may think he or she is leaving without discussing the situation because he or she doesn't want to hurt his or her therapist's feelings, or he or she fears that the therapist would get defensive. Underneath are far more possibilities as to what the real motivations for not communicating are.

Here are just two examples of the kind of dynamic that can be going on beneath the surface at such a time: Some may unconsciously fear that their therapist wouldn't care if they left therapy, and they'd rather not see that reaction when they raise the issue of leaving. Other clients who had a parent who didn't want them to leave home may imagine that their therapist also wants to hold on to them.

Don't end your therapy with a phone call, email, or text. Go in and talk about it. You've made an investment in your work and leaving without processing it may rob you of some of its greatest benefits.

It's up to you to decide when to terminate treatment, but it's essential that your therapist help you make that decision consciously, rather than unconsciously, in order to ensure that your motivations are progressive rather than avoidant. I hate to think how many people who are afraid of conflict lost an opportunity to work on one of their most difficult issues when they left therapy precipitously rather than engaging in a conscious and planned termination process.

If you're wondering whether your therapist is being helpful, speak with him directly about your concerns. If you still feel concerned after you've spoken with him, you may want to consider consulting another therapist. But I strongly suggest that you not stop working with your therapist without expressing your concerns and trying to work through them first. For a more complete description of how to end therapy see Appendix B.

* * *

One of our core principles in psychotherapy is that it's the relationship that heals. We also know that how this works out is different for everyone. But in all cases, the more authentic the relationship, and the more you can talk about it, the better.

SUMMARY

1. Be direct with your therapist about your experience with her.
2. Let her know if you feel something is being left out of your work.
3. Let her know if anything she's said leaves you angry, hurt, or offended.
4. Process any feelings that come up about the practical, business aspects of the work.
5. Notice any reluctance you have to letting your therapist be an important person in your life.

6. Explore your hopes and fears about what she thinks, who she is, and what your connection with her is like.

7. Note any similarities between what you experience with your therapist and what happened when you were younger.

8. When you're ready to go, take the time to process it with your therapist.

Chapter Five:

Be Curious, Not Judgmental:
Observe Yourself Honestly without Attacking Yourself

"Still won't start?"

"Therapy is the search for truth with empathy."
—Reverend Arlin Roy

"Honesty without kindness makes us feel grim and mean, and pretty soon we start looking like we've been sucking on lemons."
—Pema Chödrön

I suspect that most of us, if not all of us, would agree that defensiveness and self-attack are counterproductive, and that curiosity and acceptance are far more beneficial. But I'd also venture that most of us still overprotect ourselves or attack ourselves at times at the expense of curiosity and acceptance. And this doesn't change completely when we find ourselves sitting in an office with an empathic therapist. But if there's any fulcrum on which the effectiveness of therapy turns, this is it.

Psychotherapy asks that we look at ourselves with both honesty and acceptance; if either is missing, progress will be slow. But being objective and accepting ourselves is easier said than done. Here are three defensive stances that commonly get in the way:

1. "Yes, I'm bad, and if you ask me to look at myself honestly I'll just attack myself more." *Self-attack* becomes the habitual way of handling distress, and it keeps the possibility of change at a distance.

2. "I'm not doing anything wrong. How could you suggest that?" Others, due to deeply buried insecurities, use *denial* to avoid extreme self-attack. They can't look at themselves honestly or acknowledge a need to change because otherwise they'd completely devastate themselves with self-criticism.

3. "Yes, I'm doing something self-destructive, but it's better than the alternative." This is *rationalization*, a justification for questionable behavior. I find that exaggeration is often enlisted in this strategy. Rationalization has its own difficulties, but it's easier to work with.

The truth is, being open and objective about ourselves is really difficult to do, and most of us use a combination of self-attack, denial, and rationalization to avoid it; we criticize ourselves mercilessly for some behavior, and deny our responsibility in other situations. There's an emotional logic behind each of these defenses, which I'll get to soon. But first I need to explain why they're so detrimental to work in therapy.

You might think that this would be obvious and people would drop their defenses in therapy, but I can tell you that as therapists we spend a fair amount of our clients' session time trying to get the judge off their backs so that they can be objective and move ahead productively. And the process of those who can't look at themselves with honesty and curiosity tends to be glacially slow—at best.

Without both honesty and acceptance, it's hard to make progress in therapy. The two go hand in hand: without them awareness decreases and defensiveness increases. We grow the most when we're challenged to acknowledge the truth of how we're living and we rise to the challenge. Therapy that doesn't question us doesn't achieve much change. And denying our shortcomings can be more painful in the long run.

But it's also natural to have a defensive reaction when we're challenged to live differently. Go ahead and have your defensive reactions first, but then step back and look at them. Eventually you'll need to replace them with curiosity and acceptance; observe yourself honestly and accept whatever it is you see. For now. We'll get to the change part, I promise. But for now, I'd suggest that you adopt the attitude of the famous Zen teacher Suzuki Roshi, who was fond of saying, "You are perfect as you are, and you can use some improvement."

THE EMOTIONAL LOGIC OF SELF-ATTACK, DENIAL, AND RATIONALIZATION

However, since none of us can simply turn this stuff off, let's look at some typical motivations—the emotional logic—that lead to self-attack and defensiveness so that we can loosen their hold on you. I'll describe some typical motivations for each of these defenses; yours may be different. I'm giving these as examples, not as definitives. All of these show up in therapy sessions. Notice whether any of them resonate with you. If none of them do, imagine what you fear would happen if you didn't get defensive or attack yourself.

SELF-ATTACK

While it doesn't appear to be a defense at first, people sometimes use self-attack, paradoxically, as a form of protection. I'll outline four possible underlying motivations for this.

1. Self-attack is often used as a preemptive strategy: "If I condemn myself first other people will see that I know how bad I am. Then they won't attack me first, and I won't be blindsided." And in a compromising emotional logic, I can "safely" ensconce myself in a purgatory of self-disparagement. But I also become "safe" from the progress that therapy offers.

2. For other people the inner logic of self-attack as a defense goes something like this: "If I *know* that I'm falling short somehow, and I constantly keep this awareness at the center of my attention, then at least I'm not that bad." They punish themselves in a sort of compromise: "I know I'm bad, but at least I don't let myself get away with it."

3. When parents aren't able to be good enough parents, the child may develop the habit of blaming himself for his parents' inadequacies. "My parents aren't bad. I'm responsible. If I work hard enough I can make things better." That feels much safer and more powerful than feeling that the people who are supposed to be nurturing him aren't up to the task. At least then there seems to be some hope of improving the situation. Otherwise he's toast.

4. A fourth motivation, which a remarkable number of people feel is absolutely necessary, goes something like this: "The only way to keep myself from going over to the dark side and falling into a state of total and permanent laziness, indulgence, and decadence is to keep a gun aimed point-blank at my self-esteem 60/24/7/365. That's right, all the time." These people fear being let off the hook so they set up therapy as a

perpetual inquisition. The rationale is, "If I accept myself I'll become bad." Many people assume that self-acceptance prohibits growth and condemns us to mediocrity at best. While some might acknowledge theoretically that acceptance is necessary for change and would work for other people, many of them still feel that accepting themselves personally would be like bungee jumping without the bungee. Self-criticism feels like the safety cord that keeps them from falling into indulgence and mediocrity.

The result in all four of these motivations is that the judgment leads to a self-fulfilling prophecy: the lack of acceptance brings about the "failure" and suffering they're trying to avoid. And it can make therapy ineffective.

Brenda

Brenda was thirty-two years old when she came into treatment depressed after a second long-term relationship had ended. She was also upset that her career as a singer-songwriter was going nowhere, at least partially because she wasn't presenting herself well or playing out much. Brenda was, however, very good at making others feel good about themselves; she was complimentary and supportive, but she also used self-effacement, putting herself down, to make others feel good, assuring them subtly that she would not compete with them. It seemed to be a good strategy. At first.

She had no problem attracting either friends or partners, but both types of relationships eventually fell apart. As she told me laughing, "I always screw everything up. I'm not good at relationships."

It seemed that most of her friends and partners grew tired of her putting herself down because her self-deprecations never resulted in substantial change, and because they never felt that they actually got to know the real Brenda. What she tried to pass off as good-natured self-acceptance was really a pervasive and limiting pattern of self-criticism.

In our sessions I saw her engage in so much self-attack that I sensed that if I pointed things out that might be going on inside of her, or make suggestions for constructive change, it would just add fuel to the fire. And whenever I said something supportive she dismissed it with a put-down.

Eventually I said, "It looks like it's really hard for you to accept a compliment."

"You're right," she said. "Just one more thing that I suck at." She said it with her usual smile but then she became visibly saddened. "Why would I laugh at a thing like that?"

"Did it upset you?"

"Well, maybe. I think I'm getting tired of doing it—putting myself down. When I had that fight with Angie—well—maybe she was right. Maybe it can get tiring hearing somebody put herself down all the time. I think what might have been worse for her was just watching me do the same thing over and over again and never changing."

"From what you told me, I also had the impression she was frustrated because it felt to her like you were just putting up a front."

"I just can't stop it."

"Not yet at least," I suggested to her. "Let's keep being curious about this. Is there anything that feels good about putting yourself down?"

"It does feel safer. This way I'm sure they won't criticize me or laugh at me. The one time I said something positive about myself in middle school all the other girls laughed at me. I told myself I'd never let that happen again. It's just safer this way."

"Is it really?"

"Well, it didn't help me with Angie. After a while she realized that the way I laugh at myself isn't really as self-accepting as it looks. I think it's really just my mask. I wear it whenever I feel anxious. "

We went on to explore her anxiety and how she had adopted her self-effacing strategy when she was quite young. She had had an angry, critical father and a competitive but insecure mother. She learned to steer clear of her father's wrath and her mother's anxiety by putting herself down and flattering them. While she wasn't aware of fearing my anger *or competitiveness, she did the same with me. It had become a habit with whomever she was with.*

"I don't even know when I'm doing it. Tell you what—will you stop me each time I do it?"

I agreed to point it out. It happened so often at first that we were both able to find it comical. But it did help her to eventually minimize her self-effacing behavior. She had made a shift from judgment to curiosity that opened up other possibilities including a more effective way to present herself as an artist.

DENIAL

In order for therapy to help us move forward, we need to acknowledge the ways that we're living that hold us back, and to admit that the old adaptive strategies aren't working for us anymore.

The cartoon character Pogo's famous saying comes to mind: "We have met the enemy and they are us." But I don't see our inner workings as the enemy; I see them as old strategies to adapt to difficult life circumstances. These strategies may have been helpful at the time, but they limit us as we enter new stages of life. Many of these strategies were never consciously developed and have become, in effect, unconscious habits, the blind spots in our psychology. To the extent that these old strategies become conscious, they become less adversarial, more flexible, and even beneficial.

But sometimes the idea that we've been behaving ineffectively seems like a shaming accusation, an implication that our character is flawed. Then we feel we need to employ denial to protect us from shame, the sense that there's something fundamentally wrong with us. But from the point of view of psychotherapy, this is not a moral issue, but simply one of efficacy: How's it working for you? If you see outdated behavioral strategies as moral failings, it's understandable that you'd be reluctant to acknowledge them.

If you notice an immediate resistance to your therapist's interpretations this may be a clue that there's something vulnerable inside of you that you feel you need to protect. If you can, slow things down; you'll notice just before the pushback a sharp fear, a fear that things could fall apart very quickly. The use of denial usually runs in proportion to the degree of pain inside. It calls for our utmost compassion.

RATIONALIZATION

One form of defensiveness that doesn't appear so blatantly defensive and can compromise our work in therapy is rationalization. It's similar to denial, but different in that it acknowledges that something we're doing isn't optimal; it just finds a way to justify it. Rationalization likes to pose as enlightened, civilized, or commonsensical, and therefore in some ways it's even more insidious than other defenses. But perhaps worse, it keeps us from being honest with ourselves, and nothing could be more inimical to the spirit and success of therapy.

Rationalization is a form of self-deception in which we try to give a reasonable justification to ourselves for something we're doing that really isn't so reasonable or justifiable. "I know that I can't afford it, but I'll feel better once I buy that laptop. That's how I'll take care of myself." "I know that it's not good to skip sessions, but I really want to figure out what my problem is and I'm much too upset to make sense of anything this week so I'll wait until next week." "Yes, I've got a fever of 102, but I really need to get into work to get that report done because otherwise my boss will be mad at me." In each of these cases the person has some sense that what he or she is doing is self-destructive, but the person fears that the feelings he or she would experience if he or she looked at the situation objectively are just too disturbing to process, so the person tries to make it sound reasonable. At the time it's the best way he or she can manage to avoid his or her suffering.

Typically people enlist rationalization to prove that what they're doing is acceptable, and so therefore they're still acceptable as a person. I don't know anyone who hasn't used rationalization at some point in his or her life. And there may be times when we need to use it until we're ready to face into a disturbing issue.

But while rationalization may occasionally have its place, it also has its price. It actually takes a lot of energy to use, and it blocks consciousness and change. Many clients have told me that when they were young they spent more energy justifying not doing their homework than it would have taken them to actually do it. It's not much different in adulthood. The avoidance or rationalization seems worth it at first, but it ends up being much more expensive than you imagined.

Watch for clues that may indicate that you're rationalizing in session. Here are some examples:

- Justifying why you've been doing something questionable. ("A few drinks really help me to get past my creative blocks so I can paint.")
- Exaggerating circumstances to justify your behavior because you know on some level the circumstances didn't justify the behavior. ("She must have nagged me a hundred times to take out the trash, so of course I quit doing it. It really feels good to get back at her.")
- Trying to prove the inevitability of what you're doing. ("Of course no one's going to talk to me at the party, so why should I go?")

Once you start to recognize these moments, and accept them, you may actually find them entertaining: "Whoops! There I go again, rationalizing." We all use rationalization. The questions are, "How destructive is this particular rationalization?" and "Can I step back and lovingly acknowledge that I'm using it?"

Here is an example in which a client protectively used denial, and then rationalization, before eventually lowering her defenses enough to be curious about her reactions.

Jeannette

Jeannette, a forty-seven-year-old divorced sales representative, didn't like people telling her what to do. She was referred to me by human resources at her workplace because she was not open to feedback from colleagues or management. She took great pride in her work and was a respected but feared member of her team. Each year when it was time to discuss her annual review she would push back with her supervisor. Even though he affirmed her good work, she aggressively rejected any suggestions that he made about how she might improve her performance. And she didn't reserve these reactions just for her boss; she gave her colleagues the same treatment.

It wasn't long before the same reactions came up in session with me. It seemed like she felt she needed to defend her image as the perfect sales rep, the perfect friend, or the perfect client. After observing this for some time, I noted to her that whenever I suggested she might do something differently or think about something differently she became agitated.

"So what?" she asked me with a bit of an edge. "You'd be defensive too if people were always unfairly criticizing you."

"Yes," I agreed. "You're right! I would. Tell me what that's been like." And together we got very curious about this long history of being unfairly criticized.

This was a step forward: she was still defensive, but in a paradoxically self-accepting way. She stopped using denial and started using rationalization, which is much easier to work with. Instead of denying that she was defensive, she owned it. Then we were able to begin the work of empathically understanding what led her to push back when others made suggestions. It was human to want to feel good about herself and there were reasons that she felt she needed to protect her image.

She told me that her parents had always been lavish in their praise, and she wondered, with such affirming parents, why she'd feel the need to be so perfect. I asked, "Just how lavish were they?" After some exploration it became clear that their praise had been so unrealistically effusive and over-the-top that she felt she had to be brutally critical with herself to live up to their expectations. While such praise may not seem like such a bad thing, if it doesn't match the experience of the child, it can backfire.

When praise is this overstated it's actually experienced as a criticism because it doesn't mirror what the child feels and who they actually are. The praise is experienced as a standard the child can't meet without severe self-discipline. After a school theater performance in which Jeannette stumbled through a very minor part, her parents told her she was the most outstanding actor there. She knew it wasn't true and instead felt worse.

In order to cope Jeannette developed her own critical voice in an effort to live up to her parents' standards. And then to make matters worse, she imagined that others were criticizing her the same way whenever they made suggestions.

She had relied on her heroic efforts at work to prevent the criticisms of others, and to silence an underlying self-critical voice. Any suggestion that she wasn't perfect triggered a terror that she'd have to deal with her own brutal self-attacks. She eventually reassessed the standards she had unconsciously adopted as a child, and with greater self-acceptance she was able to hear the suggestions that others made to her without defensiveness.

ACKNOWLEDGING AND RELEASING THE BURDEN OF DEFENSES

So, ask yourself: How do I defend myself? What are my favorite strategies? Is self-attack one of them? Do I rationalize self-destructive behavior? What makes me defensive? What am I defending? And, how is it working for me?

There are times when it's important to appropriately defend ourselves and our reputation, and even set the therapist straight when she's off her rocker. But being habitually defensive doesn't just keep out the dangerous stuff: I can guarantee you that it's also keeping out the good stuff. This is true in a general way in life, but it's especially true in therapy. As if you were washing your hands with gloves on, the protective layer defeats the purpose.

Acknowledging our mistakes and shortcomings can feel downright awful, even if we do it without judgment. And it would be pretty unrealistic of me to suggest that you never be defensive in your sessions. But it may be possible to recognize when you're feeling the urge to defend yourself and talk about it with your therapist. If you can, that's great. The two of you can explore what it's about. I don't put too much emphasis on breakthroughs, but when they do happen, this is the kind of work that brings them on.

And letting go of the defensiveness can be a great release. Defenses are actually a heavy burden to carry. As Captain Kirk used to say in Star Trek whenever they were about to be attacked: "All energy to shields." When we realize that we don't have to prove that we're extraordinary, or even just OK, we can drop the defenses and return the energy that was going into self-protection to more fulfilling activities. To a large extent, it's really what goes on inside of us, our self-attacks and our attempts at justification, that cause our suffering, rather than what other people are saying about us.

Therapy challenges our defenses: it asks us to be honest with ourselves, *and* it serves as an opportunity to see what life can be like when we give up trying to prove things about ourselves that we don't really believe. With time honesty becomes a relief, and it clears the way for a more relaxed and productive life. When your self-acceptance is informed, that is, when it includes the acknowledgment of things you're doing that aren't so skillful, then the burden of self-protection begins to ease.

CURIOSITY

We need to replace self-attack, denial, and rationalization with curiosity. Curiosity doesn't judge or justify, it just wants to know what is. When a scientist begins an experiment, he or she may have some hope about what the results will be, but these shouldn't skew his or her objectivity. A good scientist wants to know the truth, whatever that might be.

And this isn't just about intellectual curiosity. It's about mind wide open and heart wide open, too. The etymological roots of the word "curiosity" are the same as those of caring and cure. Curiosity demonstrates a caring for the many different parts of yourself—not just the self-serving ego that wants to have everything under its own control. Emotional receptivity, an openness to know what you're feeling, scanning for whatever emotion is there, is also part of what constitutes the work in therapy. If it's hate, so be it. If it's envy, so be it. If it's pride, so be it. The "cure" comes *after* the curiosity and care.

Your therapist's interpretations are meant to stimulate your curiosity. Be curious as to any ways that she *might* be true. Even if her interpretations don't feel entirely accurate, they may stimulate ideas that hadn't occurred to you before. The entire project of therapy requires some openness to your therapist and her ideas about your inner workings. Ask yourself if what she is suggesting resonates. This may take some digging. Just saying, "I don't know" will shut things down. On the other hand, if you find yourself automatically disagreeing *or* agreeing with your therapist, that's cause for curiosity too. Slow down to check in with your gut and see what that's about.

Your therapist should be a great help in stimulating curiosity—but she can't do it all for you. Be curious about your motivations—why you've developed strategies that don't work. Be curious about what your body is saying, about who you really are rather than who you think you should be, about how you impact others, about all the other feelings that are below the one you are immediately aware of, about what you're doing that's not working, and about the truth you may be avoiding.

ACCEPTANCE

Once your curiosity leads to some insight as to what's been going on beneath the surface, acceptance needs to kick in. This may happen quite naturally: "No wonder I've been acting that way." But sometimes you may not like what you see, and then it's especially important to accept what you've realized, because it's the acceptance itself that begins to change the behavior you don't like.

Recall the story of "Beauty and the Beast." The only way for Beast to be freed from his "curse"—which is just another way of describing a painful and unskillful way of adapting—was to get someone to love him. When Belle eventually does come to love him, he's freed from the curse, and returns to his princely state. I suggest that you not take these fairy tales literally, but metaphorically: that *someone* that you get to love you and break the curse is going to have to be *you*. Think of all the characters as representing different parts of one person. The story may appear to be a sort of romance, but it's really about self-love and self-acceptance.

Call it self-compassion. Call it forgiveness. Call it the most reasonable response anyone could make given the circumstances. But know that without acceptance, you've got a painful road ahead of you.

While this might seem to support the accusation that therapy just lets people off the hook, self-acceptance is actually a requisite to seeing ourselves clearly enough that we can take responsibility for how we live. Without self-acceptance any challenges to your usual patterns serve only to reinforce defensiveness and self-attack, and then block the possibility of insight, with its ensuing emotional and behavioral change. Even if it seems like a relief, self-acceptance is part of "working on it."

Acceptance is only the starting point. And it is the *only* starting point that works. It's very different from resignation. Any artist, athlete, or entrepreneur who's succeeded can tell you that he or she would not have gotten to where that person is if he or she hadn't acknowledged his or her weaknesses. To deny or defend where that person was falling short would have ended his or her career. The same applies in therapy: to acknowledge that our old ways aren't working is where we *start*. It's not an admission of defeat.

Les Misérables

French novelist Victor Hugo's classic *Les Misérables* portrays the tragedy of unrelenting judgment and the value of generous forgiveness. The contrast serves as a model for all of us.

To make a very long story very short, Jean Valjean has been sent to jail for stealing a loaf of bread to feed his family. While in prison, Valjean looks squarely at his infraction, and concludes that while what he did was wrong, the punishment far exceeds the crime. He escapes five times, and each time he's brought back his original sentence of five years is extended. By the time he's let out, he's served nineteen years.

Once he's finally freed and out looking for work, he encounters a merciful priest whose example of compassion and forgiveness inspires Valjean to undergo a complete change of heart and behavior. But change of heart or not, society doesn't like convicts and he's forced to live under a pseudonym. Yet he still succeeds at a manufacturing business venture and becomes a generous and beloved civic leader, and a committed father to an adopted daughter.

However, the police detective Javert, whose entire reason for being is to apprehend criminals and see to it that they're punished, is always on the lookout for someone who might be guilty. Valjean is a perfect target for his obsession and he pursues him relentlessly. Javert completely ignores Valjean's reformation and generosity, and seems to experience his only satisfaction in seeking his punishment. In contrast Valjean spares Javert's life when he has the opportunity to kill him.

In the end Javert commits suicide when he realizes that it has actually been immoral to pursue punishment the way he had. After torturing Valjean and himself for decades, he realizes that there is no way out from such a conflicted approach to life.

Valjean on the other hand dies a happy man. But I suspect that what strikes most of us about the story is the senseless suffering that Javert and his judgmentalism create, and how that compares with the forgiveness and compassion that Valjean demonstrates.

Javert is alive in most of us, but to differing degrees. You might think that this quest for justice would actually make the world a better place. But here's the problem: like Javert, in many of us the part that judges has completely lost track of its real mission. He's become more interested in punishing people than in making the world a better place. He's gotten so rigid that he misses the forest for the trees.

If there's a part of you like Javert, constantly punishing you for what you may have done wrong, it's very hard to be curious, and to know who you are and what you need to change. You have to spend your life in hiding, and it actually gets in the way of doing good. Valjean, who forgives everyone, including Javert and himself, models the solution. If we apply this to our lives, we need to ask: Who holds more sway inside of us, Javert or Valjean?

SUMMARY

1. Notice and say when you feel defensive about the possibility of doing things differently.
2. Don't attack yourself for using old, ineffective adaptive strategies.
3. Be honest with yourself: watch for instances in which you feel you need to rationalize your behavior.
4. Replace judgment with curiosity. Be very curious about what's going on inside of you, including your motivations for self-attack, denial, or rationalization.
5. Accept who you are now as a starting point.

Chapter Six:

Carry Your Fair Share, and <u>Only</u> Your Fair Share:
Differentiate When to Take Responsibility and When Not To

*"Protect your family, protect your yard, and
stop obsessing about port security."*

"I am not what happens to me, I am what I choose to become."
—C. G. Jung

Frederic

*Frederic, a fifty-year-old single musician, had come to therapy to try to
get out of a deep and long-standing depression. His mother had been an*

extremely anxious woman, and he imagined that he was the cause of her distress. So from a young age he tried to soothe her anxiety by being well-behaved, attentive, and affectionate. It actually helped him to soothe himself when he thought, "Surely if I behave better, she'll calm down." However, it led only to placing harsher and harsher expectations on himself to behave well, because he wasn't responsible for his mother's anxiety. But without this belief in his culpability, he would have felt totally powerless and helpless—which was worse than feeling guilt for supposedly bad behavior.

He went on to apply this strategy to all of his adult relations and ended up quite depressed from the weight of responsibility.

One day Frederic walked into his session and commented that I looked tired. I asked him what he imagined had made me tired. He thought for a moment, and told me, "As soon as I saw you in the waiting room, I thought that telling you how upset I was last session might have been too intense, and that you got tired just thinking about seeing me today. I told myself that I should be sure not to make this a difficult session for you."

"What would that mean?" I asked.

"It would mean showing progress, but also giving you something easy to work on." He was planning to take care of me as he had his mother.

Exercising curiosity, we explored the many times that he had felt he had caused others distress, and the different ways he tried to make up for it. It was true that at times he had an impact on how the people close to him felt, but he didn't really control their mood. He had felt some relief in imagining that he had the control, but it was exhausting him, and he had to admit he was the one who really felt tired. He also had to admit that his efforts at control actually put people off.

Frederic did have responsibility, but it wasn't what he had imagined. His real responsibility lay in seeing what he got out of imagining that he could fix other people's moods, and letting go of it. It wasn't easy to let go, but as he did, it was replaced by relief and the awareness that he was taking responsibility for himself. And, not coincidentally, his depression began to lift.

When curiosity and self-acceptance are in place, you're in a position to impartially sort out where to take responsibility and where to let go of it so that you can move ahead. The appropriate acceptance of responsibility and the appropriate refusal of it are essential to "working on it," and to healing and growth.

People sometimes caricature psychotherapy as encouraging us to take a passive victim role and blame our parents and everyone else for our problems. Nothing could be further from the truth in good therapy. Taking too much responsibility can lead to depression and anxiety, but not taking enough leads to interpersonal problems and disempowerment. And to make things more complicated, most of us take too much responsibility in some places and not enough in others. Discerning our fitting share of responsibility is part of what makes therapy effective.

We began to explore this area in Chapter Two when we discussed the field of research known as "locus of control"—the extent to which we believe that we can control the events that affect us. Some people believe that their lives are largely controlled by external factors, while others believe that they have within themselves the capacity to determine most of what happens in their lives. In effect this also determines what we take responsibility for and what we don't. Originally it was thought that the more locus of control we felt we had, the better our sense of well-being. But with time it's become clearer that an appropriate sense of control and responsibility—one that mirrors the reality that some things are in our control and some are not—is most helpful in achieving an overall sense of well-being.

RESPONSIBILITY AND BLAME

First let's sort out just what responsibility is and is not. The word responsibility is often used interchangeably with the word blame, but for our purposes, they aren't the same thing, and they certainly have different effects. Blame, whether it's directed toward ourselves or others, usually has the tone of finding fault, the goal of doling out punishment, and a focus on the past. Responsibility, as I'm using it here, is more about understanding our role in situations in order to think or behave differently as we move forward into the future.

Carrying your share of responsibility empowers you, while blaming others can leave you feeling victimized and powerless. Responsibility helps you to understand what you can do differently, while blaming others leaves you stuck. The stereotypical image of therapy clients blaming their parents is an unfortunate misconception. We've learned through research and clinical experience over the last one hundred years that how our parents raise us does have an effect on our well-being. But this information should not be misused: no parent or pair of parents can possibly give us everything we need to live wholeheartedly, and eventually we need to come to terms with what they were and weren't able to do for us.

I've known some people who needed to go through a period of acknowledging that they *have* been angry and still *are* angry at their parents inside. The point is not to make anyone *become* angry at their parents or other caretakers, but to be more conscious of what anger *is* and *has been* there, and how that anger affects their responses in the present. Once the anger is acknowledged we can begin the empowering work of understanding how we adapted to the problems of childhood, and what we may have done to compensate for what was left out or what went wrong. The strategies that we developed to deal with our environment may no longer be serving us well, and taking responsibility for shifting those may well be life-changing.

Denise

At the age of thirty-two Denise had already started her own residential electrical contracting business. It wasn't easy being a woman in the field, but she liked the challenge. However, the business was surviving rather than thriving: when customers questioned her about work she'd done, she sometimes became defensive, and it wasn't helping. She also had difficulty building relationships; she had acquaintances, but no close friendships. She participated in a twelve-step program, and her sponsor suggested that she get some therapy since she was having a hard time getting along with people.

She had grown up in a tough family in a tough neighborhood, and her father had been determined to prepare her for an unforgiving world. He loved her a great deal and spent time teaching her the electrical trade. He was trying to help her, but he was so critical that Denise ended up feeling criticized not just for what she did, but for who she was. The result was that in order to protect her self-esteem Denise often ended up in power struggles with him, and she felt that if she ever took responsibility for mistakes she lost the battle.

Denise became so insecure that she felt she needed to maintain a mask of complete competence, and she couldn't acknowledge when she had done something wrong. Given her experience with her father and in her neighborhood, she had reason to be protective, but her strategy left her blaming everyone else for her problems and cut her off from the relationships that could otherwise have been healing.

Denise's process with me was a very gradual one, composed of many, many small episodes in which she felt that I was blaming her for something, and she recognized that she wanted to blame me in return. She eventually learned to ask me whether I was blaming her, and we were usually able to diffuse the situation. During this process she kept remembering her interactions with her father in which she usually felt accused of being stupid and of being a slacker.

On one occasion during our work she was telling her father about a problem she had with a customer on a complicated job. He could tell from what she was explaining that she could have done something differently and he started to explain it to her.

She felt herself tense up right away—emotionally and physically. She felt criticized and she wanted desperately to find some way to get

97

out of it and blame someone else—especially him. She recognized her pattern of counterattacking from our work in session: she wanted to tell her father, "I wouldn't have screwed it up if you had told me the right way to do it in the first place." Recognizing the pattern, she paused rather than accuse him. She asked, "Are you saying that I screwed up?" He said he wasn't blaming her for it; he just wanted to show her a way to do it that the customer might have liked better.

Denise's work entailed seeing that while her father did a bad job of relating, he was doing the best he knew how to teach her how to live in a demanding world, and, that while acknowledging her anger at him was important, blaming him for her own struggles would not help her. While he may have been critical of her, it was her choice how to live in the present.

With time and intention she was able to stop repeating his critical voice in her head, and to pause before responding to others defensively. She was also able to question her assumption that to take responsibility was to lose a power struggle. In fact, she realized, owning responsibility made her stronger.

DUE TO CIRCUMSTANCES BEYOND MY CONTROL

Irvin Yalom, an existentialist psychoanalyst and popular author, maintains that taking individual responsibility for our lives is an essential aspect of effective therapy. He suggests that when we say, "I can't" we need to question whether we are really saying, "I won't"; that when we say, "I did it unconsciously" we ask, "Whose unconscious is it that did it?"; that when we say, "He really bugs me" we get it right and say, "I let him bug me"; that when we say we "find ourselves" in a terrible situation we ask, "How did I create it?"; and finally, that when we hold our parents responsible for our problems we acknowledge that what we are really saying to our parent is, "I will not change until you treat me differently than when I was ten years old."[1] In effect, he's saying we need to permanently delete the phrase, "due to circumstances beyond my control."

But taking more than your fair share of responsibility by blaming yourself for things that are out of your control is no more helpful. For some this habit developed early on as a strategy to cope with a painful situation.

In Chapter Two I encouraged you to look deeply inside yourself for the *solutions* to your problems, not necessarily the *cause* of the problem. It's helpful to remember, "The person is not the problem, the problem is the problem." Whatever strategies you developed to cope are the problem, not you yourself.

THE SPECTRUM OF RESPONSIBILITY: NO, YES, AND THE GRAY AREA

But how do I decide what I am and am not responsible for? For the most part I am going to leave this to you and your therapist to work out, but I'll suggest a basic orientation, because this will affect how you approach your sessions.

I would suggest that you view the field of responsibility as a spectrum with those things that you clearly cannot control and therefore shouldn't take responsibility for on one end, and those things that you can clearly control and therefore should take responsibility for on the other end. In the middle is a gray area—things you can't immediately control, but with intention and commitment can eventually change.

On one end of the spectrum are the passing thoughts and feelings that arise quickly and unbidden. These thoughts and feelings come and go and are generally not subject to our control, so it would not make sense to take responsibility for them. Nor should we try to control them, as they often bring valuable information that may fill out an otherwise unbalanced conscious position.

On the other end of the spectrum is the behavior that we can clearly and immediately control. Don't throw the tomato soup.

In the middle, the gray area, are behaviors that are difficult to control, entrenched moods (e.g., ongoing depression, anxiety, or resentment), and aspects of thinking that are more enduring (such as beliefs, perspectives, and attitudes). These all tend to grow when we nurture them and die out when we starve them. With time, intention, and practice, we can disengage from unhealthy ways of living in the gray area so that we widen the area in which we can reasonably take responsibility.

A Cherokee legend describes the issue well:

An aging grandfather is speaking to his grandson about the battle that goes on inside of the hearts of all humans. He tells his grandson, "There are two wolves battling one another inside of us. One is fearful and angry, and the other is understanding and kind." The young boy then asks, "Which one will win?" His grandfather smiles and says, "Whichever one we choose to feed."

This is a great story, with one caution: don't beat up on yourself when you feed the wrong wolf. You might come away from this story thinking that it's easier than it really is to control which wolf you feed. This is the right direction, but adopting an ultimatum to feed the right wolf *or else* would be feeding a different sort of wolf, the wolf of judgment and blame.

One other component of this gray area is the feelings of others. We need to be aware of how our actions impact others, without taking full responsibility for their mood. Again, there is a spectrum here. Parents do have immense responsibility for their children's well-being, but that diminishes as the children mature. And to take too much responsibility for the feelings of other relatives, coworkers, and friends won't work well for any of you.

Now let's explore what to do with that gray area—the behaviors, enduring moods, and thought patterns that we can change over time.

Behavior: Confronting Complexes

In Chapter One we discussed the importance of bringing all your different personality parts into session. If not consciously integrated, one or more of these different parts may gather so much energy that they develop into independent personalities referred to as complexes. These complexes, such as the hero complex, the savior complex, the inferiority complex, or the victim complex, can develop a will of their own, hijack the rest of the personality, and make you do things you later regret.

For instance, you might have developed a particular type of hero complex in which you imagine that you can work eighteen hours a day at your social service agency job without complaints from your family or your body. When it's time for you to leave work and get back to your family and get some rest, you'll find ten reasons why you have to stay at work—none of them valid. Your relationships suffer as does your health. You know there's something off about your behavior but you find it really difficult to change. You'll need to figure out what part of you needs to play the hero and find a better way to satisfy that need so that it doesn't take over your behavior.

With time, effort, and intention it is possible to face these complexes consciously, understand what emotional needs they represent, and find healthy ways to meet these needs, so that they become less rebellious and less destructive. Otherwise you become a victim of your own psychology.

Even when the rare and extreme condition known as dissociative identity disorder (formerly multiple personality disorder) leads to different personality parts taking over behavior completely, the individual needs to work toward taking responsibility for his or her actions.[2] This call for responsibility serves as a model for the majority of people, whose different personality parts are not so dramatically independent.

Mood: Changing the Emotional Climate

Many clients are aware of the impact that their mood has on their ability to function and on those around them. They have asked me if they could will themselves out of a depression or persistent, disabling anxiety. We can't simply and suddenly will ourselves out of an entrenched mood, but we can gradually work ourselves out of it. Mood falls within the gray area on our spectrum of responsibility. Deep-seated as it may be, improvement in mood is possible but, again, it takes time and intention. With the persistent use of the tools in this book and the help of your therapist, issues of depression and anxiety can become less disabling over time. If your mood is severe and debilitating, it may be necessary to take medication in addition to working in therapy. But with or without medications, setbacks are likely, and working on it includes self-acceptance. Don't get demoralized by the setbacks. Consider yourself a work in progress.

Belief, Attitude, and Perspective: Altering Thinking

Our enduring patterns of thinking may not change immediately, but with time we can shape them so that they are more realistic, healthy, and adaptive. Low self-esteem—the belief that we are inadequate, for instance—can be changed over time if we are vigilant about challenging the unrealistic ideas we've held about ourselves, if we understand what role they have played for us, and if we allow ourselves to be open to the healing aspects of the therapeutic relationship.

* * *

All of the tools in this book work together to help you gain control of your behavior, mood, and thinking. With time, it's as if you're standing on a train platform and you get better and better at recognizing which train is coming and which one you want to get on. "Oh, that's the negative-thought train. Nope. That's the anxious-feeling train. Not that one either. That one is the act-out-your-resentment train. No way. Oh, here comes the one I want, the one that will take me to happiness and fulfillment. I'll get on that one." We'll discuss the steps to these decisions in more detail in Chapter Nine.

Ordinary People

The film *Ordinary People* tells the story of teenager Conrad Jarrett, whose psychological work and healing entailed sorting out what to take responsibility for and what not to take responsibility for. Conrad has survived a boating accident in which his older and more popular brother has died. They'd been sailing when a storm set in and his brother drowned. Conrad becomes depressed and is hospitalized after a suicide attempt. Once he's out of the hospital, he continues to suffer from depression and post-traumatic stress disorder. Since his brother was their mother's favorite, Conrad already had issues of low self-esteem. But the depth of his depression can't be accounted for solely by his mother's narcissism, or by her preference for his brother.

Conrad begins attending therapy twice each week with the genuine and straight-talking psychotherapist Dr. Berger. He also develops a friendship with fellow student Jeannine, who affirms and supports Conrad. The concern and respect he experiences with his therapist and his friend both interrupt his depressive way of thinking, but not enough to turn things around completely.

Then he finds out that a friend from the psychiatric hospital where he had been hospitalized has committed suicide, and he's devastated. He believes that he might have been able to prevent it if he had called her more often. This leads to a cathartic session with Dr. Berger in which he faces down his guilt not only for his friend killing herself, but also for having survived while his brother drowned. He explores why he felt that he needed to take the responsibility for both of their deaths, and then releases the responsibility. He also begins to assume responsibility for his own ongoing depression and begins to feel free to live again. His task was to look squarely at himself and see what he was doing that prolonged his depression. This had been his gray area, that which had seemed out of his control, but with intention and attention he was able to begin to take control of it.

CHECK OUT YOUR MOTIVATION

If you really want to get at the root of these issues so that they don't spring up again, you need to ask, "Why do I invest so much in taking either too much or too little responsibility? What do I get out of it?" This is a specific example of detecting the underlying motivations we discussed in Chapter Three.

While it usually isn't conscious or obvious, we often get something out of our maladaptive behavior, whether it be punishing ourselves or taking too much responsibility. Perhaps it's a sense of virtue in being hurt, controlling others around us by being out of control, holding on to the hope that someone else could rescue us, or the security in knowing that we're being tough on ourselves. In any case, acknowledging these motivations, finding better ways to meet the underlying emotional need, and then letting go of the old maladaptive strategy, can be life-changing.

MAKE YOUR OWN DECISIONS

One specific way that you will need to take responsibility is to take the risk of making your own decisions, including those you bring into therapy. It can be very tempting to ask for your therapist's advice rather than take responsibility for your decisions. Asking your therapist to tell you what to do in concrete situations may seem like you're just being open to wisdom, and that what you need is not change but good advice. But this won't prepare you to go out on your own eventually and develop the skills you need to navigate a course based on your own wisdom.

Your therapist can help you make decisions by exploring what makes particular decisions difficult, but also what may make the general process of decision making difficult for you. The two of you can use these situations to help you identify the psychological reasons that decisions are challenging for you, and to help you find your own inner resources to make those decisions. Therapy is much less about putting things like advice into people, and far more about drawing out of them the wisdom that lies within.

If you find yourself wanting your therapist to tell you what to do, that's a good time to slow down and explore that with him or her. In the long run, any particular decision may be less important than clarifying the process of deciding *how* to decide. This brings to mind the old saying that it's better to teach a man—or a woman—to fish than to give him—or her—a fish.

Each of the tools that I'm outlining in this book lead to the kind of self-understanding that improves decision making: taking into account all the different parts of yourself so that whatever you decide to do will be sustainable; understanding how the particular ways that you handle your feelings affect your decision making; identifying the stories you believe that tend to skew your decisions; and clarifying the values that give you a foundation with which to make your decisions. The responsibility is yours, but you need not be alone with it.

SUMMARY

1. Identify the situations where you take too much responsibility.
2. Identify the situations where you don't take enough responsibility.
3. Foster the attitude and intention to take responsibility for behavior, feelings, and thinking that you can come to control with time. Until those things are under your control, exercise self-acceptance.
4. Explore what purpose it has served you to take too much or too little responsibility.
5. Elicit your therapist's help to become conscious about how to make your decisions, but not to make those decisions for you.

Chapter Seven:

What's Your Story?
Identify the Recurring Themes and Fundamental Beliefs That Guide You

"You've got to _want_ to connect the dots, Mr. Michaelson."

"Our personal legend becomes our reason for being."
—Paulo Coelho, *The Alchemist*

In *The Story of the Eldest Princess* by A. S. Byatt,[1] a young woman, the firstborn of three princesses, is sent on a quest for a silver bird to heal her parents' troubled kingdom. She's instructed to stick to the road, to not go into the forest or the desert, and to be courteous to everyone. She sets out on a journey to save the kingdom.

Now this princess has done lots of reading and she can recognize a fairy tale when she hears one, and this is definitely a fairy tale she's living in. She knows how tales of this sort always end: the first two siblings fail in the quest and turn to stone, and the last sibling turns out to be the heroine who saves the day. She can see that she's caught in a story that's not going to turn out well for her. So she sits down on a large stone to have a good cry.

And that's when her own personal journey begins. She rejects the fairy tale and becomes the author of her own story.

Instead of pursuing her doomed heroic task to save the kingdom, she agrees to help a scorpion, a frog, and a cockroach, all in some distress, and she leaves the path she was supposed to follow. Instead she seeks the house of the wise woman, where they can all be healed. After passing through trials they eventually make it to the charming little cottage where the princess feels at home and lives her own life.

She never goes back to her parents' kingdom. We later learn that the second sister successfully made the heroic quest to retrieve the silver bird and save the kingdom, and the third sister found and pursued her own personal quest.

There are certain stories, certain life scripts, such as The Heroine, The Clown, The Victim, The Misfit, and The Caretaker, that we can all easily fall into without realizing it. Once the eldest princess becomes aware of the story that she seemed to have been forced into, she's able to make conscious decisions about how to live her life, rather than get pulled into a story that wasn't going to work for her. The story of the fairy tale heroine is only one of many patterns we can fall into, and they aren't all bad. With consciousness we can choose the roles that are authentic to us and that give our lives meaning and direction.

* * *

One of the fundamental tasks we need to accomplish in therapy is to step back from the isolated details of our lives and get a sense of the larger picture, the patterns and themes that comprise our stories and to some extent define our lives. We need to identify these stories because they lead to our fundamental beliefs about who we are, how the world operates, the nature of relationships, and what will make life fulfilling for us. These beliefs in turn lead to how we feel and how we behave. Put simply, bad stories make us sick and good stories heal.

While we do need to discuss the individual events of our past and our present, if we don't ask what larger themes recur, and which core issues consistently cause us trouble, we could spend a lifetime in therapy looking at individual events as if they were unrelated and not make progress toward a more satisfying future. Just as the eldest princess did, we need to sit down on our rock (which for many of us means going into therapy), and put the individual pieces together to discover the story that we're living in.

This tool resembles the zoom device on a video camera: it helps us to narrow in on the details at times, and then zoom out at other times to get the big picture and the patterns that emerge. It has a satisfying rhythm of going from the specific to the general and then applying it back to the specific challenges that we encounter.

In this chapter we'll explore how zooming out can help us to see the larger picture and connect the dots of our life story so that we can see the enduring themes that may not only affect us, but even control us. Rather than approach therapy situationally, discussing singular events in isolation each week, we need to think characterologically, observing the persistent themes that make up our personality and direct our behavior, leading to suffering or to fulfillment.

We'll see that these themes often follow common, archetypal patterns of experience, like the stories found in mythology and literature. We often get pulled into these patterns, sometimes for the worse, but ideally they guide us into fulfilling lives. It will be helpful to observe whether your story resembles any of these archetypal stories, and whether these stories help or hinder you.

You may notice that you often come back to the same themes in your sessions: "We talked about this before." Yes, and we'll probably talk about it again. And again. This isn't necessarily bad; in fact it's probably a good sign. Ideally you and your therapist will identify the key issues that you need to work through and revisit them, not in an endless circle, but in an upward spiral, in which you view them from a different angle each time, and find better ways to respond to the themes.

In this chapter we'll first explore why our stories are important, then we'll discuss some of the patterns that often come into focus, and then we'll explore some ways to identify our stories. In Chapter Eight we'll go on to explore what to do about these stories once we've identified them. I'll be using the term "story" loosely: for some it may be a simple phrase ("I will always fail"), while for others it may be more of an epic. Feel free to use the term as it works best for you.

THE INEVITABILITY AND NECESSITY OF HAVING A PERSONAL STORY

We all create stories about our lives and our world. We seem to need to make sense of what's happened in the past and what's happening now. Our stories help the brain to organize and recall incredibly complex information, and they lead to the beliefs that help us to navigate the world without having to reassess each new situation individually.[2] Sacred texts such as the Bible, the Mahabharata, and the Koran have used stories to serve as the foundation for beliefs about how to live. But we all develop beliefs from the stories we cultivate, whether they are spiritual or secular. The question is whether we do this accidentally or with conscious intention.

The quality of the stories that we develop impacts the quality of our lives and relationships. Having a cohesive autobiographical narrative gives us a strong sense of a core self that helps us to be resilient in the face of challenges. Using words to construct our story helps us to build the neural networks that we need to contain emotion and use it effectively.[3] It also affects the quality of the attachments we form with others, including our children.[4] This process of constructing or reconstructing an accurate story of our lives is one of the tools that we use in therapy to help us bring about change.

The story that we tell ourselves about the difficulties we face will affect how we interpret those difficulties, and how well we navigate them. As we'll explore in Chapter Ten, whether the story you tell yourself is one of possible breakdown or breakthrough will lead you to either despair or inspiration. Ironically, we sometimes organize our lives around stories of despair, and over time even come to defend them and perpetuate them as if our lives depended on them.

Stories are powerful medicine. And, like any powerful medicine, they can help or harm, depending on whether we take the right one in the right dosage. They can either create or diminish energy. Whether we are aware of it or not, we're always taking this medicine, always telling ourselves as being stories, with both helpful and destructive consequences. Sometimes we take too much, sometimes we take the wrong medicine, and sometimes the medicine is just plain bad, tainted in an unhygienic laboratory.

One of the reasons that stories are such a powerful part of our lives is that they engage images and imagination, both of which bypass more logical functioning. No matter how reasonable we might like to think of ourselves as being (which is in itself a story), these stories have a magnetic influence that's hard to escape.

We all tell ourselves stories about how we've come to be who we are and where we're going. It is the default mode of the brain.[5] Some of it's true, some of it isn't, and some of it we'll never know for sure. But having a story is still necessary. You're going to do it anyway, so you might as well develop one that's true and helpful.

UNCONSCIOUS AND MISLEADING STORIES

We usually create the first editions of our stories when we're too young to do it consciously, so they often end up playing in the background, influencing us constantly without our being aware of it. And they may be inaccurate and unhelpful; they may put more emphasis on certain events and leave out others, creating a skewed sense of reality, which leads us down some very painful paths. Further, if current reality doesn't fit in with our story, we might not register what's really happening or even deny it. Then we're stuck, unable to take in the new information that could change how we live.

If, for instance, the essence of my story is that my family gave me a bunch of anxiety genes and sent me on my way, and that my only hope to feel better is to get rescued, I might not notice when I *am* able to calm myself down. I might not register the many things that I *have* done independently to take care of myself. What doesn't fit my narrative is excluded; I engage in a self-fulfilling prophecy, and a downward spiral ensues. I don't utilize the capacity for independence that I actually do have.

PATTERNS IN OUR STORIES

Some of the themes and stories that guide our lives are our personal versions of universal themes that have been developing for thousands of years. These themes describe patterns of behavior that originally had some adaptive, evolutionary value for the species. For example, we've needed both leaders and followers to form the communities that have helped us to survive. Exaggerated versions of these stories lead some to become tyrants and others to become so submissive they can't think independently when they need to. Others may adopt a story that guides them to lead or to follow in a way that is fulfilling for them and their community.

Another axis of patterned behavior concerns openness to relationship: we have needed both alliance and self-protection to survive. You might fall into exaggerated patterns that lead you to either isolating independence or unhealthy dependence, rather than healthy interdependence. These patterns are described in literature, mythology, and folklore, in which cultures and individual authors have condensed wisdom about these themes in an attempt to give guidance for our individual journeys.

That these patterns exist is both a blessing and a curse: they can function as superhighways that speed us to where we want to go, or as ruts in the road that limit our mobility. Being aware of these possibilities can be helpful in getting us onto a path that's more satisfying.

These patterns, and the way we respond to them, have been described from many different angles in both psychology and literature. Some examples of the ways that these patterns have been described in psychology include attachment styles,[6] core conflictual relationship themes,[7] archetypes,[8] schemas,[9] complexes,[10] and scripts.[11] While there is much overlap between psychological and literary approaches, for clarity's sake I will first discuss the themes that have been identified more through psychology, which tend to look back, and then I'll describe those that have become apparent through literature, which more often guide us forward.

ATTACHMENT STORIES: LOOKING BACK

One of the main stories we live from is what it's been like to get close to people. From this story we develop beliefs about the best way to relate to them. This story forms very early in life based on the quality of attachment, the bonding we had with our primary caregivers, and is then generalized to all other people. Current psychological research, by analyzing videos of mother–infant interaction in frame-to-frame detail, is clarifying the important role that early attachment to caregivers has in the quality of our life as adults, in effect outlining the typical stories that we tend to develop about relationships.

Through this research three main attachment styles—three main ways of relating to others—have been identified: secure, avoidant, and anxious/ambivalent.[12] Other additional styles have been described as autonomous, dismissive, enmeshed, and disorganized. The stories and their ensuing beliefs go something like this:

- Others were dependable and responded to my needs, so it's safe and good to attach to others (secure).
- Others were distant or disengaged, so it's best that I take care of myself and not get close to others (avoidant).
- Others were inconsistent, intrusive at times, and distant at others, so it's best that I stay reluctant to get close, yet protest with upset when others leave (anxious/ambivalent).
- Others have not been safe or predictable, so it's best to dismiss them (dismissive).
- The people I needed to depend on were dangerous, so it's best that I dissociate from my intolerable feelings. As a result, I can't develop any particular way of relating (disorganized).
- Others were not dependable, so the best way to handle it is to cling to them (enmeshed).

Identifying the story that you developed about getting close to people and the beliefs that resulted from that story can help you to know what you need to focus on in therapy. But this cannot be an intellectual exercise. You'll need to let yourself feel and express emotion about many different relational episodes before you try to understand the pattern. These episodes could involve parents, siblings, lovers, friends, coworkers, children, and your therapist. The results of this exploration will be less beneficial if your emotions aren't engaged.

Aaron

Aaron was anxious and somewhat isolated. A single, forty-two-year-old researcher for a large biotech firm, he wanted relationships, but also felt very wary of them. In our sessions he would report the week's events to me in detail each week. His reporting was somewhat pressured, which made it hard for me to get a word in. But then again, I wasn't sure he wanted me to get a word in. The result was that he kept me at a distance. At first it was hard for us to see any connections between the many different episodes and situations he brought in. But as we explored what happened between us, and started to connect the dots of his experience, his story started to come into focus.

I told him, "You seem to have a lot to say, but I also wonder whether you feel uncomfortable with me saying anything." He thought about it and replied, "Well, yeah, I do like to have control of the sessions."

"Come to think of it, this reminds me of what I talked about two weeks ago, about how I got really annoyed when my neighbor asked me to turn down the volume on my stereo. I mean, it was eleven o'clock, but I think people should be able to do what they want. I wanted to tell her off, but you know me—I don't do that kind of thing. Anyway, when that lady in HR told me I couldn't take vacation in May, I got annoyed again. And now that I think about that, it used to drive me crazy when my mother used to get in my face at first, and then make me stay in my room. It's like nobody's gonna let me do what I want." Aaron was starting to connect the dots, relating the various episodes he brought in to a central theme. But he still distanced himself from the issue intellectually. He had moved on pretty quickly from the emotion at hand, his fear of my impact.

"And does that happen with me?" I asked him. This time he took the chance and stayed with it. *"Yes. I don't want to feel that you or anyone else has an impact. I can't tell you how disturbing that is. It's like I'm just going to evaporate if it happens. I want you to help me, but I don't want you to help me. I want to do it myself."*

Aaron began to see, and feel, the outlines of his story: "People will intrude on me, control me, and prevent me from doing what I believe in, so I need to stay clear of them." It colored everything he experienced, and even led him unwittingly to try to prove that his story was true, to prove that others were holding him back. Based on what he told me about his mother's intrusiveness, and my own experience of him wanting to keep me at a distance, I gathered that he had developed an anxious and ambivalent attachment style, one that made him want to get close to people but also led him to avoid relationships for fear of losing his autonomy.

When he connected the dots a larger theme became clear, and he was able to question his story and make better decisions about how to expand his life without the old story limiting his possibilities. It also brought to light the fact that his story had been incomplete: it did not describe what he needed freedom for, what it was that was so important for him to accomplish that he had to keep other people at a safe distance.

Aaron had been overprotective of his autonomy. Once he slowed down enough to pay attention to his anxiety rather than avoid it, he began to understand that his isolation was a skewed attempt to protect his independence and his unique talents. His anxiety brought his attention to the fact that something was being left out: part of him longed for a more creative and fulfilling life than he was allowing himself.

Eventually he changed jobs to one where he was able to enlist his creativity more. As the result of his work in therapy he could begin to explore what role his independent thinking had to fill in the outer world, and to live from a less protected and more satisfying narrative. He also began dating.

PERSONAL MYTH: LOOKING AHEAD

As important as our stories of attachment are, they aren't the only stories we tell, nor are they the only ones we need for emotional health. Attachment stories tend to look backward, they help us to understand where we've come from and, once understood, help us to form better relationships. But we also need stories that lead us forward, guiding us to what we need to pursue in order to find meaning and fulfillment in life. Without them we're using a rearview mirror to drive into the future.

For thousands of years the stories of religion and mythology helped us to maintain our sanity and gave us direction in life. But for many the older religious stories no longer have meaning, and myth is equated with inaccuracy. In effect, many of us try to live without stories.

But whether we are aware of it or not, and whether they are secular or spiritual, we all have guiding stories that serve as belief systems. In their very condensed form they lead to beliefs such as, "Once I have enough money I'll be happy," "Meaning and fulfillment is to be found in service," "If I work hard enough I'll be loved," "The right partner will solve my problems," and "Nothing is really worth striving for. It's all futile anyway." Some of these stories work for us and some of them don't.

Sometimes we slip into powerful archetypal dramas without knowing it. Some live out a hero theme, identifying as Hercules and trying to use their strength to crush everything that gets in their way. Others may identify with Cinderella, the long-suffering martyr who does all the dirty work with the hope that Prince or Princess Charming will someday come to the rescue.

We all have a belief system, in effect a religion, which has a huge impact on our mental health, and we're much better off when that belief system is consciously chosen. For our purposes here, the issue is not whether it includes God or life after death. The question is whether it works for us. While for some the old cultural stories no longer feel relevant, many people find that a personalized version of a deeper, more universal pattern helps them to feel more grounded, more connected to their own roots.

As we discussed in Chapter Three, there is something that motivates you to do whatever it is you do. The question is whether you are aware of those motivations, and whether you've chosen those motivations consciously. These motivations are driven by the stories and beliefs out of which you operate. These may be traditional religious ones, or decidedly nontheistic ones such as science or hedonism or freedom. It's not your therapist's job to tell you what to believe, but ideally the two of you will clarify what beliefs you do operate from. Until you're clear about this, someone's pulling your strings.

Put differently, the stories we tell ourselves lead to our values and principles. If the story you've told yourself is that the world is a dangerous place in which you have little control, self-protection and survival will become your supreme values. Fulfilling relationships, satisfying creativity, or the simple joy of being present and savoring the moment will all be left out.

On the other hand if your story is one in which resilience and perseverance lead to fulfillment, there's much more room to pursue things that are valuable to you, and then you've got a very different sort of life in front of you. Working on it in therapy includes sorting out what gives your life meaning, and finding a set of values that works well for you. Without this work you'll be vulnerable to all sorts of influences, many of which may not work for you.

HOW TO IDENTIFY YOUR STORY

Exposing your underlying story requires connecting the dots to see what themes are consistent in your life. These dots include the many different life episodes that you've brought into therapy, your dreams, your experience with your therapist, what gets you annoyed, resentful, angry, or fearful, and what moves you, excites you, and gives you pleasure. Observing your interactions with coworkers, family, and friends outside of session, and watching for patterns in how you react, will be very important. You may also find hints in the themes and characters in your favorite (or least favorite) movies, television programs, fairy tales, books, or songs. Look for the elements or themes that are common to these different aspects of your life.

For instance, let's say that you start to notice that many of the episodes you talk about in session are about trust. Here are some questions to ask:

- Do those episodes imply that you trust too easily or only with great difficulty?
- Do you let others in too quickly or are you often suspicious?
- Use your own experience of your therapist as an additional clue to understanding your story: Has it been easy or difficult to trust her?
- Ask your therapist: What has been her experience of you in terms of how trusting you are?
- Have you had any dreams that touch on the issue of trust?
- What literature has moved you?

Perhaps your fascination with the film *The Matrix* is informative: the hero realizes that he needs to question whether he and everyone else has been duped into believing they are living a satisfying life, and throughout the film he is trying to figure out whom he can trust.

Now, put these all together and take it a level deeper:

- What story have you been telling yourself about people that's led you to feel that way?
- In your life narrative, what happened to get you to that place?
- What does your story say about the value of people in your life?
- Going forward, have they become important in an unhealthy, dependent way, or not important enough?

You can apply this tool to any other subject that appears to be a recurring theme in your life: work, pleasure, the body, suffering, pain, vocation, awareness, death, or food. Identifying the story underneath the theme helps you to stop identifying *with* it, and opens the possibility for changing it. Once you know the story, you're no longer the problem. The problem is the problem.

Meredith

Meredith, a documentary film producer and mother of three, had a different story to tell me each week about how other people were breaking the rules, about her efforts to correct them, and about her frustration when she couldn't correct them. She was determined to make the world a better place no matter what it took. She was right about people's shortcomings in many of her stories, and she was remarkably adept at spotting the things that other people were doing wrong. But her approach wasn't bearing much fruit, and the real question she needed to ask herself was, "Why am I so obsessed with other people breaking the rules?"

Meredith had taken her son to see the movie Divergent, *which describes a post-apocalyptic Chicago where the citizens are divided rigidly among five factions: Dauntless (the protector warriors), Erudite (the thinkers), Abegnation (the selfless), Amity (the peaceful), and Candor (the truth speakers). Meredith knew immediately that she would have fit right in with Candor. They saw things in terms of black and white, right and wrong, and had no patience for the softer, peace-loving approach that others felt led to social stability. The skills of Candor were essential in the community's judicial system. In that image, Meredith was relieved to see not only her identity, but also the purpose behind that identity. Her truth telling had meaning.*

But the film also illustrated Meredith's story and the problems it caused: the society had a strict rule that characters who didn't identify themselves rigidly with one of the five factions, with one exclusive role, were to be shunned. Meredith had unknowingly adopted that rule; she believed that Candor was to be valued above all, and it was her role to identify exclusively as a sort of prophet. The result in both the film and Meredith's life was power struggle and vehement conflict.

Even though she wasn't at all a religious person in the traditional sense, Meredith had identified with the role of the prophet for much of her life. The role of the prophet is an ancient theme found in many religions and mythologies; it describes the member of the community who has the role of pointing out what's wrong. People play this role in many settings outside of religion: policemen, quality controllers, thesis committee members, and football referees. While there is value to the role, it had completely defined Meredith. It had become a burden and had destroyed many of her relationships.

Meredith found relief only when she was able to see the recurring theme of her life and the identity she had assumed. She looked at the pattern of the material that she brought into sessions, and put it into the context of a larger story. She was then able to find a specific place where her "prophet" energy could be used productively so that it did not have to take over her life completely.

Your story may not be as obvious as Meredith's, and you may have more than one story that guides your life. If it appears that you have no story, that's very useful information in itself and may help explain the struggles that you're experiencing. But assuming that you do have a background story, write it out, first in depth and then in a very succinct way, so that you can identify it quickly when you begin to get caught in it. This will also prepare you to create a more accurate and useful narrative as we'll discuss in the next chapter.

SUMMARY

1. Watch for patterns and themes in the issues that most affect you and that you bring into session most frequently. If it seems that there is no connection among the issues you bring in, ask your therapist for help in identifying your patterns.

2. Zoom out to see the big picture, the overarching patterns in your life, and then zoom back in to see how it plays out in the details.

3. Note if these themes surface in your relationship with your therapist, in your dreams, or in the stories that catch your attention.

4. Identify and write out your dominant stories and beliefs, both looking back to early attachment issues, and looking forward to issues of meaning.

5. Ask yourself whether these stories are helpful or destructive.

Chapter Eight:

It Ain't Necessarily So: Build a Better Narrative and Choose Your Beliefs Consciously

"Openness to questioning one's assumptions, especially when they are self-defeating and incorrect, is a key predictor of positive outcome in psychotherapy. Once clients begin to understand that what they assumed to be reality is actually a personal fabrication, they either flee or become fascinated."[1]

—Louis Cozolino

"In this nineteenth century, the religious idea is undergoing a crisis. People are unlearning certain things, and they do well, provided that they learn this: There is no vacuum in the human heart. Certain demolitions take place, and it is well that they do, but on condition that they are followed by reconstructions."

—Victor Hugo, *Les Misérables*

I promised you when we spoke about responsibility and change in Chapters Five and Six that we'd get to the change part. Here we are. Responsibility is a call to action, a call to change both our thinking and our behavior. This chapter will explore the thinking that eventually leads to behavioral change: challenging the stories we've told ourselves about ourselves and our world, and constructing new ones that are more accurate and helpful, and lay the foundation for behavioral change, which we'll explore in Chapter Nine.

I've heard many people ask, "What good does insight do?" Insight—understanding *why* we live the way we do—opens the possibility of thinking and behaving differently. Without it, change is likely to be short-lived. But while insight is a necessary step for change, it's not by itself sufficient. This chapter will help you to take the next step: thinking differently and creating a new story that sets the foundation for behaving differently.

Phil

Phil, a single thirty-six-year-old computer programmer, lived in a persistent state of low-level anxiety and mild depression. Things weren't terrible, but they'd never been good either. His parents had lived very restricted lives, careful never to aim too high with their careers or to go into debt. It seemed as if their entire life strategy was one big insurance policy, always holding something back to make sure that they'd be safe. He recalled that when he got excited sometimes they'd tell him, "You're flyin' too high, young man."

Phil thought that he had avoided their fate. He had pursued a career that interested him and afforded him some financial cushion so that he could travel occasionally, trying adventures such as skydiving, motorcycling, and hang gliding. He assumed that he had overcome his parents' self-imposed limitations, but with each exploit he tried he became more and more aware of a deadness that no adventure would cure. Eventually he had to question whether he had really escaped his parents' overprotected life. He came to learn that he had done so only on an external, concrete level.

There was another, deeper assumption that he still shared with his parents that he hadn't become aware of; he assumed that if he really let himself be happy, or if he really let himself feel good about himself, something terrible would happen. He had not challenged the psychological aspect of their strategy; if you're too happy, or if you feel too good about yourself, you're sure to experience a devastating fall.

Phil began to realize that he had unwittingly and somewhat incorrectly adopted an idea from the ancient story about the Greek character Icarus. He recalled images from a picture book he'd seen when he was a boy: when Icarus flew too close to the sun, the wax that attached feathers to his arms so that he could fly had melted and he fell into the sea. The story he had pulled together from this image and his parents' example had led to an assumption: if I fly too high, if I feel too good, I'll crash and burn. Skydiving had been his unconscious way to try to overcome this fear.

To challenge the assumption, Phil had to first slow down and let himself feel more deeply than he usually did, past the surface level of minimalistic expectations, down to old hopes and disappointments, and into his fears of falling emotionally. Once he let himself feel the deep sadness and longing that he had been avoiding for much of his life, he could also see and feel the emotionally protective role that his caution had played for him. He recognized a sequence of emotion: hope, fear, and deadening, all in relation to hopes about himself, hopes that had not been unrealistic.

He began to question his old beliefs about pleasure and pride. Phil looked up the story of Icarus and noticed that he'd left out an important part: Icarus's father had also warned him not to fly too low. Somehow this part didn't register with him, though: it didn't fit in with the story he had adopted. He decided that while there were no guarantees in life, even if he did fly a little too high and took a fall, it would not be as bad as the quiet desperation that flying low left him in. If he did fall into the sea he could swim to shore.

With time Phil began to develop a new story, including the belief that he might actually be able to live more happily and more confidently without experiencing a devastating fall, and that he didn't have to fly so low after all. He was able to build this new story by beginning with dream fragments, exploring and expanding on images of himself that conveyed expansive feelings totally unfamiliar in his waking life. These images bypassed his overly rational approach and offered a new attitude from which to live.

Phil's work serves as a model for the eighth tool: once he identified his story, he questioned it and then constructed a better narrative. To do this he enlisted tools that I've already described: he asked what parts of himself were left out, he focused within, he listened to the feelings of sadness that told him something was out of balance. He noticed that he was afraid of what I'd think of him if he felt good about himself. He was very curious and resisted the temptation to blame himself for being foolish. He pulled all of these pieces together and challenged the idea that he had to fly low. And then he developed a better story, one that led to beliefs that allowed for a richer life.

CHALLENGE YOUR ASSUMPTIONS

Assumptions grow out of the stories we tell ourselves, and, if we don't examine them for accuracy, they can lead to the more overarching beliefs by which we live our lives. For example, if my story is that I was treated badly as a child, I may assume that people treated me badly because I was somehow lacking. Once I accept that assumption, it will seem "logical" to then believe that I shouldn't trust anyone to treat me well since it's all my fault anyway; I'm inadequate.

These assumptions can *appear* to be reasonable; we're unaware that at some point we adopted them even though they may not be based in reality. Becoming aware of the assumptions that lead to beliefs, and determining which ones are helpful and which ones are not, is a fundamental aspect of the work we do in therapy that helps us to change.

Assumptions aren't necessarily wrong. They may be accurate and help us form beliefs that work well for us. But some of them, as protective or comforting as they may seem, are erroneous and self-destructive.

I've already described one example of this: the assumption that change comes only through self-attack. This assumption may have initially been adaptive if your parents tried to control your behavior with severe punishment; if you could preempt their attack with self-attack, you avoided the pain of being attacked by your parents. Or it may have been adaptive with a parent who was detached and gave no guidance; you may have needed to keep *yourself* "in line" because you had no idea what was needed to get along with others. But beliefs about how to behave that may have been adaptive in the past can prevent growth and healing in the present.

Stories, assumptions, and beliefs are actually closely intertwined and can be hard to sort out. My point is not to differentiate the three, but to give you some sense of how to untangle the story you've been living. Stories, assumptions, and beliefs may all need to be challenged in order to make change. Here are some questions that can be helpful:

- What and who are the sources for the stories I have told myself?
- Are they reliable?

- Is it possible that in that early context I misinterpreted situations?
- Does my story lead me to globalized or generalized thinking, thinking that the rest of the world will be just as my early circumstances were?
- What are the assumptions that I've made based on those stories?
- Have I developed "all or nothing" thinking?
- Are my old ways of adapting working or not?

Memory is extremely plastic and notoriously unreliable,[2] so you may need to question whether your memory is as accurate as you've assumed. To begin to develop a more accurate picture we can ask some of these questions:

- What are the exceptions and the events that don't fit in?
- If that old story is true, how is it that things have happened that don't fit in with it?
- Is there a more likely explanation?

For instance, are things still the way they were when you were a child? One of the assumptions that most of us struggle with is the assumption that the future will be just like the past, and that people in your current life will treat you as your parents did. If you're assuming that everyone else will indulge you as your father did, you've probably already run into some rude surprises. On the other hand, maybe they'll be more forgiving than your parents were.

The therapeutic setting offers an opportunity to observe, question, and, when necessary, release the convictions that drive our lives. It often creates the type of experience that we don't acknowledge because it doesn't fit into our old stories. So, one of your jobs will be to notice and acknowledge those events in therapy that don't fit into your story so that you can begin to create a new story. As you notice these events ask yourself what they say about how you think of yourself and how you relate to others.

Pauline

Pauline, a forty-five-year-old administrative assistant in a midsize corporation, was certain that no one at work liked her. She thought of herself as someone who was direct, and assumed that people at the office didn't like that. But as we explored her past, she began to acknowledge that this wasn't just situational: she had felt that way just about everywhere she went, even though there were indications that some people had liked her and cared about her. As she began to think more in terms of her character, and less as if her current episode was the main issue, she started to see her pattern and her story.

Perhaps more harmful than believing that no one liked her, she told herself that she didn't care whether they liked her or not. Her parents had cared about her, but they had been so preoccupied with a perpetual list of emergencies that they didn't take the time to check in with her to make sure that she was OK. Meanwhile, she had become the victim of intense bullying at school, and the best coping strategy she could find at the time to protect herself was to feign indifference. She even convinced herself that she didn't want people to like her.

Our work together provided ample opportunity for her to experiment with her assumptions. She let me know when my interpretations were off. She let me know how she felt about the decorations in my office. She let me know that she could see when I wasn't sure what to say. Each time this sort of thing happened I could honestly say that I appreciated her being direct with me, and that directness enhances relationship. This didn't match her expectations: it didn't fit in with her belief that no one wanted to know what she felt. She also began to recognize an old and deeply buried hope that someone would want to know.

While she knew that as her therapist I played a different role than most people do, she was willing to risk seeing me as a real person, so that after a fair number of these experiences she could begin to question her assumption that people wouldn't like a truth-teller. She was also able to question her half-truth that she didn't care what people thought. The whole truth was, she did want me to like her, and she didn't need to stifle herself to make that happen.

As Pauline questioned her old assumptions, she was able to consider new possibilities, including the possibility that she could be liked, and that she might actually enjoy that. Her new story ran something like this: Because of what I've been through I'm not a mainstream person. I see things differently and that has its challenges and its benefits. I'm like the trickster coyote in Native American legends—I shake things up. But my role and my differences don't have to keep me separate from others. Not everyone is going to like me, but some of them will appreciate my differences if I don't push them away. If I like them too, then I can choose to be a friend or a partner.

LETTING GO: THEMES OF DEATH AND REBIRTH

Letting go of the old stories isn't always easy. They may seem like they've been faithful companions or caretakers[3] for much of our lives, and creating a new story may feel as though you're betraying them. You might even feel like you're losing your religion; sometimes we make our defenses into spiritual systems, and the defense seems sacred.

Here's one of those places that stories from literature can serve us with their guiding function. Virtually all cultures have their own legends showing the necessity of death for the possibility of rebirth: the phoenix, the mythical bird that builds a nest to set itself afire and reemerge anew; the old king who must die in a yearly ritual to fertilize the fields; the hero who undergoes resurrection or rebirth; the snake that sheds its skin; and the seed that dies in order for the plant to grow. All of these stories provide comfort and inspiration for a process in which the ruling, dominant attitude must be replaced by one that is more suited to a new situation. Some of the beliefs that we've held most important in life may actually be the beliefs that keep us from feeling better and living more satisfying lives. Letting them die is a natural part of life.

Empty the Teacup

A professor once consulted a Zen Master and asked him to explain the meaning of Zen. The master quietly poured a cup of tea. When the cup was full he continued to pour, with the tea running onto the table and down to the floor.

The professor was stunned and demanded, "Why do you keep pouring when the cup is full?"

"I want to point out to you," the master said, "that you are similarly attempting to understand Zen while your mind is full. First, empty your mind of preconceptions before you attempt to understand Zen."

ADDING STORIES TO DEVELOP BALANCED PERSPECTIVE: CYCLOPS VISION AND BINOCULAR VISION

In some cases, though, the story and beliefs we've lived from are true to some extent, but are incomplete. In situations like this we need to be able to adopt additional, balancing beliefs, and not necessarily relinquish the one we started with. For example, if one of your guiding beliefs is that hard work pays off, you'll need to balance that with a belief in the benefits of savoring leisure and play, or there won't ever be any payoff.

Notice that humans and virtually all animals have two eyes—two distinct but cooperative viewpoints from which to view the world. When combined, these two perspectives give us an accurate and balanced view of the world. When I was a child and my parents took my brother and sister and me to the New Orleans Wax Museum in the French Quarter, our favorite figure was the swamp monster, a

Cajun version of the Cyclops, a one-eyed giant also found in Greek mythology. He was big and hairy, but the really scary thing about him was that one eye. There's reason for that: having just one way to see everything is pretty dangerous and leads to some really awful behavior. It's unbalanced, disturbed, and disturbing.

Another version of the monster with a skewed way of seeing things is the one with its two eyes on opposite sides of its head. In this case there are two different ways of seeing things all right, but these two are so far apart that they can't be brought together so that they balance each other. The problem with some of our life stories is that they consist of two completely separate and conflicting narratives: the eyes are so far on each side of the head that they're unaware of each other, and the story is split into two opposing ways of seeing life.

One week (or one minute) we feel one thing and the next week (or minute) it's something so completely different that we can't even remember what it was we were so excited about before. For example, we've all heard of the inferiority complex: One eye tells the story, "Everyone else is better than me." But the eye on the other side of the head says, "I'm much better than everyone else because I'm capable of incredible things." The two eyes need to cooperate to create a more balanced and useful story.

BUILD A BETTER NARRATIVE

The neurological underpinnings of psychological change rely on the creation of new neural networks to either override the old ones,[4] or complement the ones you have. But what are the sources of the new story? Clearly you can't just make something up void of reality: the new story needs to take into account the limits of your genetics, your history, and your environment.

The sources of a new story may come from many different places. Yours may be unique, but I'll describe some common ones here:

- Seek fulfillment: What story would bring the most pleasure and meaning to your life?
- Borrow wisdom: What stories (myths, novels, films, for instance) inspire you?
- Follow your dreams: Are there themes in your dreams that point to a more helpful story?
- Make gold out of lead: What direction have the challenges of your life pointed you toward? (I'll say more about this in Chapter Ten.)
- Make necessity the mother of invention: Do your current life circumstances force you to adopt a new story?

Your new story doesn't have to be elaborate or written in stone. Ideally it will include a sense of where you've been, what you believe is most important in life, and what you believe the best way to live going forward will be. It should stand as a reminder, a basic guiding principle, when things are difficult. It can change as your circumstances change, but at the same time it shouldn't be so flimsy that the slightest wind knocks it down.

PERSIST IN CREATING NEW NEURAL PATHWAYS

Don't worry if you can't shake the old story right away. It takes time and some repetition to build new neural networks that override or complement the old ones. You may need to be persistent in building a case for a different life story, focusing on different evidence rather than trying to prove the old story. My experience is that implementing a new story tends to be a gradual, incremental, and accumulative process. When you're first making a change, in a given week you may operate out of an old story 60 percent of the time and the new story 40 percent of the time. But with intentionality—a conscious determination to think and behave in a specifically different way—next week that balance can shift in favor of the new story.

More and more often you'll notice when you are at a fork in the road in which you can choose whether or not to operate out of old assumptions. You will need to resist the tendency to take the old road; push back against the old story, and take the new road, living out of the new narrative:

- "No, I'm not really a jerk. We'll all be better off if I treat myself with respect."
- "No, I don't really need to use cocaine to feel good. I have better ways to feel good."
- "No, I don't have to give in to what he (or she) wants from me. I can set appropriate boundaries and still not be all alone."

Notice that in each of these examples, the person is not only saying "no" to old unhealthy behavior, but also saying "yes" to a new story about how to live.

You won't get it right all the time, but each time you do, you strengthen the new narrative. There is no real magic here, but if your new story is realistically conceived, perseverance in living out of a new set of guiding principles will lead to the change that you've wanted.

As Einstein said, insanity is doing the same thing over and over and expecting different results. Therapy provides an opportunity to closely observe the repeating patterns in your life, to have different experiences with your therapist that challenge the old assumptions and stories, and to experiment with different responses that grow out of different stories.

SUMMARY

1. Challenge your assumptions; question whether or not the things that you have believed are true. Is there any evidence? What emotional needs might have led you to hang on to the old story? Is there a better explanation?

2. Let go of old stories that don't work. Have a ritualistic funeral for them if necessary. (I'll say more about this in Chapter Nine.)

3. Develop a balanced perspective; add stories to the ones that already work for you.

4. Play with other possibilities. Enlist imagination.

5. Note which stories of literature inspire you and then make them your own.

6. Persist in adopting the new story. Push back when the old beliefs come up, and push forward with the new story.

Chapter Nine

Do Something! Continue Your Psychological Work outside of Sessions

"Today we're going to talk about lowering the drawbridge."

"Perhaps all the dragons in our lives are princesses who are only waiting to see us act, just once, with beauty and courage. Perhaps everything that frightens us is, in its deepest essence, something helpless that wants our love."
　　　　　　　—Rainer Maria Rilke, *Letters to a Young Poet*

You can make progress toward change, taking responsibility, and integrating a new story by working both in and out of session. Work outside of session includes observing the patterns in your life and thinking about what meaning they have. But deep change also requires moving beyond thinking to action—applying the insights you've had in session by doing things you haven't done before. Taking action has the added benefit of helping you to feel less helpless and more capable. Whatever you're working on, you can do something about it.

Extending the work beyond your therapist's office also serves as a bridge to completing therapy, and to continuing the work after you stop attending sessions. Good therapeutic practice prepares you to work independently eventually, and ideally you begin building bridges to work on your own while you're still in therapy. Therapy should feel safe and relatively comfortable, but not so safe and comfortable that you aren't motivated to try new behavior. It should never collude with attempts to escape from life, but rather should serve as a way to deepen and broaden your involvement in it.

Action outside of session can take many forms. I'll outline them in four broad categories, but they all overlap:

- *Complementary Work:* Exercise, meditation, support groups, group therapy, etc. You can supplement your therapy with health-oriented activities that support what you're working on in therapy.
- *Outer Work:* New behaviors that apply the insights and the new story to your outer life. This may include planning specific *assignments* with your therapist to help you gradually achieve your goals, or developing more general *intentions* that lead to spontaneous changes in behavior.
- *Inner Work:* Journaling, creative projects, active imagination, and dream exploration. This type of work may not seem as "active" as outer work, but because you're doing it on your own, and because it can have powerful results, inner work is definitely a way of taking action.
- *Symbolic Work:* Ritual and ceremonial actions that take place externally and have a huge effect internally. These outer actions represent inner change, demarcate a new way of living, and can be a potent way to solidify the gains you've made in

therapy. While the value of ritual and ceremony are largely dismissed today, research shows they can actually serve a very practical function and can help you to make a demarcation between living from an old story and from a new one.

In this chapter we'll explore how you can extend the psychological work that occurs in session into your world outside of therapy, discussing each of these four ways of taking action. Choosing what will be most effective for you will require looking at your particular concerns, and finding a balance between comfort and challenge. We'll explore both the fear and the courage that can arise when we transfer personal insight to life in the outer world, and when we investigate our inner world on our own. But first let's look at a few ways to boost the work you do in therapy.

COMPLEMENTARY WORK

You can supplement your work in therapy with other practices that contribute to your emotional health in a general way and that approach your issues from different angles. I won't explore these possibilities in depth because plenty has already been written about them. But I do want to affirm that other approaches can support and enhance the work that you do in therapy.

- *Exercise:* The psychological benefits of exercise (including yoga) are immense, improving both mood and cognitive functioning.[1] It also helps to connect you with your body in a positive way.
- *Meditate:* Whether you consider yourself spiritual or not, meditation can help you to feel better and make your work in therapy more effective.[2] Any form of meditation that increases awareness and acceptance *without repressing feeling* can be helpful. In particular I've found that the systematic,

moment-to-moment practice of self-acceptance that meditation espouses is very useful in applying Tool Number 6, being curious without judgment. Mindfulness-Based Stress Reduction,[3] for example, is a form of meditation that requires no religious beliefs and has been shown by extensive research to be very helpful in achieving improved mood and health.

- *Engage with others in community:* While spending time on your own to reflect is healthy, isolation is not. Whether you choose a religious community, a motorcycle club, a writing group, a volunteer group, a sewing group (my mother-in-law used to enjoy a group called "Stitch and Bitch"), or a group of people who simply have similar interests, you'll be better off having a group of people who share your perspective and support you in your goals. If there is anything more healing than therapy, it's community.
- *Join a support group:* Twelve-step programs and other support groups can be combined very successfully with psychotherapy. They can reinforce what you work on in session and provide additional support when you aren't in session. If, for instance, you want to lose weight, you're much more likely to succeed and remain successful if you do it with others.[4]
- *Participate in group therapy:* Group therapy can be helpful in gaining insight and getting feedback from others about how you relate and come across in ways that you might not be aware of. It provides experience that individual therapy may not be able to offer.
- *Attend workshops:* Opportunities to engage in creative therapies can be found in workshops using psychodrama, dance therapy, music therapy, and other approaches. You can take the themes that you've identified in therapy to work on there, and bring back the themes you discover in the workshop to your therapy sessions. Workshops that include bodywork may also be helpful for some to mend any splits between the body and the spirit.

- *Take a test:* Many have found the use of a personality assessment tool such as the Myers-Briggs Type Indicator (http://www. myersbriggs.org/my-mbti-personality-type/take-the-mbti-instrument/index.asp) helpful to understand, accept, and work with their specific, personal disposition. Even if you disagree with the method or results, it can stimulate new ways of thinking about your personality and deciding what will work best for you.

- *Read:* In conjunction with psychotherapy, reading books about the specific issues you want to address may be helpful, *if* it's not just an intellectual exercise. If you want to read for healing and growth, feel it and apply it.

I suggest that you speak with your therapist to see which, if any, of these supports may be helpful in your specific situation. One thing to keep in mind with these suggestions is that it's best to have only one psychotherapist. To have more than one can dilute your process and cause conflicts. You don't want to set up a situation where the therapist who tells you what you want to hear becomes the good guy and the other one who challenges you ends up being the bad guy. The main exceptions to this are group therapy and couples counseling, in which you may have a second therapist in a different role. Still, it's best to be aware of the possibility of splitting, pitting your two therapists against each other.

OUTER WORK: ASSIGNMENTS AND INTENTIONS

When clients ask me to give them assignments for work outside of session, I work with them to develop a plan that will help them to face into their challenges and to apply the insights we've been working through. Any homework that's planned is best developed specifically to fit your own style, and developed organically out of the specific work that you're doing with your therapist.

Compare your goals with how you actually behave. If your behavior is not going to get you where you want to go, you may need to develop a set of steps, progressing gradually from relatively comfortable to much more difficult, to help you arrive at the behavior you want to engage in. Perhaps more important than completing those steps is becoming aware of the feelings that make the change in behavior difficult. Bring those feelings into session and explore them with your therapist to see what's getting in the way of change.

But formal and specific "homework" assignments as such need not be a part of psychotherapy. The work of changing behavior as a result of your experience with your therapist and the insights you've gained can also happen spontaneously once you've developed an intention to act differently as opportunities arise. Here are some examples of clients acting on their intentions:

- Intention: I don't want to lose control so much.
  - ◦ "I made it a point not to yell at the insurance guy on the phone."
- Intention: I need to communicate more directly.
  - ◦ "It was hard, but I told my sister that I was angry at her."
- Intention: I need to be more realistic.
  - ◦ "I set up a budget and I've stuck to it."
- Intention: I need to take care of myself better and be less controlling.
  - ◦ "I finally let myself buy a new mattress after sleeping on the old one for fifteen years."
- Intention: I need to be more self-disciplined and procrastinate less.
  - ◦ "I put in an extra hour of studying."
- Intention: I need to listen to my body more.
  - ◦ "I let myself just soak in the bathtub for an hour after work."

- Intention: I don't want to let my fears control me.
  - "I was afraid of riding in the elevator, but I did it anyway."
- Intention: I want to be less reactive.
  - "I felt hurt by what he said, but instead of reacting I decided not to assume I knew what he meant. I asked him what he meant and it turned out it wasn't what I thought."
- Intention: I don't want to feed my depression.
  - "I felt like saying, 'The hell with everything,' diving back into my depression and eating the whole carton of ice cream, but I went for a long walk instead."

Insight and behavioral change are reciprocal and mutually reinforcing. A relatively small insight may allow you to change your behavior, and that change of behavior, through a specific assignment or more general intention, may lead to more insight. Watch the following sequence:

- "I needlessly and excessively worry what other people think about me." (insight)
- "I'll take a chance and wear what I want to the party." (behavioral change)
- "Most people didn't even notice, and even if anyone didn't like what I wore, I survived. No—I didn't just survive, I really liked wearing what I wanted to wear. I had been needlessly frightened of being shamed and rejected." (insight)
- "I won't keep spending time with people I don't like or doing things I don't enjoy." (behavioral change)
- "I'm so much less depressed and so much happier when I do the things I like and don't do the things that I don't really need to do. That's what I did to please my parents and avoid feeling like I'd be abandoned." (insight)

- "I'm leaving the job where I was treated badly and paid poorly. It was prestigious, but I don't need the status anymore." (behavioral change)

We can increase our understanding and change our feelings to some extent by changing our behavior.

Or, as another example, if you drink because you feel insecure you've probably realized that drinking doesn't really raise self-esteem—even though it may feel like it briefly. In fact, drinking may *reinforce* low self-esteem after twenty minutes or two hours or two days, if it's been a long binge. On the other hand, if you've been preparing yourself in therapy by understanding your patterns, each time you refrain from drinking you gain more experience handling life soberly, your confidence and self-esteem increase, and you feel less need to drink. Positive behavior reinforces itself. Because of this no change is too small to make a difference.

The Hobbit

Bilbo Baggins, the unlikely hero of Tolkien's *The Hobbit*, wants nothing to do with the quest—a sort of assignment—that the wizard Gandalf calls him to at the beginning of this epic. Comfortably ensconced in his peaceful hamlet and beautiful home, he can see no reason to leave at first. But something inside of him longs for adventure. Something in him longs for more than a regular schedule and a comfortable armchair.

Once he decides to go, the challenging events that require action on his part each serve to bring out parts of his personality that had not been developed before, especially his strength and heroic capabilities. As Gandalf says of Bilbo, "There is a lot more in him than you guess, and a deal more than he has any idea of himself."

We can read *The Hobbit* as the story of a man who goes from being a passive complainer to an active leader. The more he takes action, the more he changes. In one of the early episodes he and the dwarves discover swords, lost for years, which were renowned for their role in killing goblins. These swords represent his capacity to stand and fight, but also discrimination, separating out what has value for him from what doesn't, and developing his own values apart from those of others. He uses his sword to free himself and his comrades from the webs that huge spiders have used to capture everyone in the expedition. This action, this accomplishment, is self-reinforcing; it leads to an increase in self-esteem and confidence that allows him to take on greater challenges.

Bilbo takes an increasingly important leadership role in the expedition as it gets closer to the treasure they seek, and as the dwarves become more stubborn and reckless. He *has* his feelings rather than the feelings having *him*, and this allows him to use his feelings as a guide for his action. In fact it's Bilbo's clever actions that eventually help save them from the dragon and recover the lost treasure.

We can interpret Bilbo's journey as either outer work or inner work, but in either case he faces down the dragon, takes its strength and courage, and makes them his own. For many of us, working on it in therapy means that we leave the comfort of a limited life. Whether this leads us to an adventure in the outer world or the inner world, it often leads to experiences that could feel dangerous to us. Like Gandalf (though hopefully not *too* much like Gandalf), the therapist invites the patient to a world outside of his or her comfort zone where parts of his or her personality that had lain dormant can emerge.

* * *

The tendency for some is to wait until they feel comfortable before trying to change their behavior. I suggest that you not wait. The process of therapy, your relationship with your therapist, and using all of the tools I've listed here *will* loosen the grip of your old story and make it easier to behave differently. It's *not* just a matter of willpower. But you could be waiting a very long time if you expect therapy to *completely* remove your anxiety, sadness, or anger. Instead, "Fake it 'til you make it": act differently from how you feel and eventually it will change how you feel. In some cases new behavior needs to precede feelings rather than follow them.

Putting yourself in circumstances that have been uncomfortable and gradually exposing yourself to the things that you fear can eventually increase your comfort zone. For example, if you're shy, introduce yourself at a meeting. If you struggle with commitment, stay in a relationship a little longer to see if it's viable. And if you're perfectionistic, try letting your work be a little less perfect.

Some fear that if they fail in their efforts to do something new, it will only set them back. The truth is, most of us tend to exaggerate the downside of failing: we "catastrophize," rationalizing not trying new behavior with the excuse that it could make us feel worse. Research in the field known as post-traumatic growth indicates, however, that people usually handle crises, not just setbacks, much better than commonly expected.[5] And, as we'll discuss in Chapter Ten, crises are often the occasions for our greatest growth.[6]

In the introduction I made reference to therapy being more like physical therapy and less like massage. In physical therapy, the therapist determines which muscles have atrophied and gives you exercises to strengthen those, so that other muscles don't become injured when compensating for the weak muscles. In similar fashion, the process of therapy aims to strengthen the muscles of your psychology that have not been exercised. Much of that happens in session, but ideally it also happens outside of session.

Sarah

Sarah was a fifty-seven-year-old married, recently retired schoolteacher. She'd come to therapy because she was depressed and she had a tendency to depend too much on others for constant reassurance and advice. She had witnessed her mother die of a heart attack when she was eleven years old. While she had received plenty of support afterward from her warm, caring father and two supportive aunts, the loss still had significant effects on her, including her depression and a reluctance to do things on her own.

She and I had worked together for some time and she had made significant progress in improving her mood. But we were also aware that she was still too dependent on her husband, and that without consciousness on both our parts she would simply transfer her dependence from him to me rather than move independently into the larger world.

We explored her fears about taking more initiative and doing more things on her own. We discussed how these fears had shown up in our sessions; she'd wanted me to start the sessions for her, to give her advice about what to do with her life, and how to handle her interactions with her father and aunts. In each case we explored her fear of making her own decisions and living more independently. We had also explored some of her motivations to get her husband to do things for her; she felt that it was proof that she was loved. By this point she was aware of the story she had been telling herself, and tentatively constructed a new one. But it still felt abstract to her.

So rather than me giving her assignments, we worked together to help Sarah outline a list of actions for her to take outside of our sessions that would help her to gain some initiative and independence. She set some specific and incremental goals for socializing and volunteering, including calling the local hospice service, and going to their orientation. She also developed a more general intention: to follow her own lead rather than look for others to give her guidance.

Sarah completed the assignment she had set for herself by attending the hospice orientation. As soon as she arrived she noticed that she wanted to find someone to tell her what to do. Should I sit? Should I stand? Should I read all of this material on the table? But she resisted the temptation to depend on others for direction, and instead worked on her more general intention—to follow her own lead. She took the chance *of doing what she thought was the best thing to do. These were small steps but they were encouraging to her.*

After the orientation, Sarah felt just comfortable enough to commit to training to become a hospice volunteer. Once the training began, she noticed her dependency tendencies again; she wanted the trainers to tell her exactly what to say to the people she visited with. They were able to tell the class what not to say, but this still left Sarah with many decisions to make on her own once she started visiting.

Sarah was able to use the hospice visits as opportunities to stretch beyond her comfort zone, processing with me the feelings that came during her visits. She took chances doing what seemed best to her at the moment and learned that her natural sensitivity could serve her well when she trusted her intuition.

With these victories, and engagement in volunteer work that she found profoundly meaningful, she was gradually able to feel more comfortable following her own lead, and to do more things independently of her husband, which also increased her self-esteem and improved her mood. She found community with other hospice volunteers, and when she left therapy she had made healthy relationships that sustained her and gave her great pleasure.

INNER WORK

Actively exploring your inner world on your own may be just as life-changing as outer work, and may be even more of a challenge for some. By *inner world* I mean the thoughts, feelings, and images that are below the surface of everyday awareness, but which have a huge impact on how we feel and live. Ways to approach this inner world include journaling, making art (poetry, visual art, music, or dance), using imagination in an active and direct way, and working with your dreams. This inner work may not feel natural for all of you, and it isn't a requisite part of psychotherapy, but it can be a very powerful way to continue the work on your own.[7]

Journaling

Keeping a journal, or just about any form of writing, can deepen the work that you do in therapy,[8] and simply writing about your feelings has been shown by research to yield both psychological and physical benefits.[9] I'm not referring to the type of journaling in which you mechanically record what you do every day in a diary. The kind of journaling I'm referring to can be either a further investigation of the themes you discover in your sessions, or freer writing that explores whatever feelings arise as you write. Journaling has the advantage of being totally private so that you can express yourself without fear of shame: some things are more easily written than spoken. You can decide later whether you want to share the results with your therapist or anyone else.

For many, writing serves as a way to focus and to follow a thought or a feeling without getting distracted. It can be particularly helpful when identifying the different parts of your personality, when trying to stay with a feeling and seeing what it has to offer, and when sorting out old stories and starting new ones.[10] Research indicates that it can be therapeutic to process traumatic events through writing[11] when used in conjunction with psychotherapy.

Journaling can be used to further work on any of the tools in this book. Here are some things to write about to get you started:

- What are the main parts of my personality, and which ones exert the most power?
- What have I wanted to hide? Is there anything I'm leaving out of my therapy?
- What feels unresolved from my past?
- What am I feeling in this very minute? What hurts? What feels good?
- What keeps me from living as I want to live?
- What story have I lived from in the past and what story do I want to live from now?

But writing spontaneously—with no particular direction or goal, and no censoring of any sort—may be just as rewarding. Writing freely may be just as helpful in giving the excluded parts of you a chance to express themselves, and in opening the channel between your gut and your head.

Some people find it helpful to write letters that they don't intend to send in order to express anger, sadness, or longing, or to achieve a sense of closure and let go of resentment. In order to release the old story and its pain it may help to write a letter to the people who hurt you, express your feelings, and eventually accept that the person who hurt you probably won't change.

Developing comfort with journaling will serve you well once you leave therapy. Many find that after sessions are over, their journal becomes the place for letting all the different parts of their personality speak, for expressing, containing, and learning from feelings, and for updating their narrative.

There are many books to help you with therapeutic writing. Two that you may find useful are *The Therapeutic Potential of Creative Writing: Writing Myself,* by Gillie Bolton,[12] and Dennis Slattery's *Riting Myth, Mythic Writing: Plotting Your Personal Story.*[13]

Creative Work

Just about any creative pursuit could be used to further your psychological work. You can paint a mood, sculpt a personality part, or dance a story. What would you see if you looked deeply within and painted a portrait of your mood? Who would emerge if you sculpted the part of your personality that you've been afraid to let out? What would happen if you let yourself move expressively without reservation? What would your shadow sound like if it could make poetry or music?

Your creations may be more directed and specific, or more spontaneous and free. Drawing or making a collage of your family often reveals a great deal about roles in the family and can shift your perspective. Drawing a mandala (an elaborate circle) may help you to get centered. On the other hand, starting with a spontaneous squiggle and then allowing yourself to draw freely may take you places you never expected to go. Many people find that using their nondominant hand in any of these exercises allows them to be more spontaneous. Creating art may also be a way to express feelings or experience that's been impossible to do with words. This may be the case especially if you have experienced trauma, loss, or other crises that have led to overwhelming or complex emotions that have been hard to put into words.

Work of this sort is intended to bypass our more linear thinking and to let the unconscious express itself, perhaps allowing pain to surface, but also ideally accessing the wisdom that the unconscious has to offer. It isn't about making great art; in fact its benefit has more to do with the *experience* of making it rather than with the finished product, with being freed from rules and expectations, and with allowing yourself to experiment with self-expression that's new and very personal. It allows the unconscious to speak; it allows aspects of your personality to come to the fore that had no other way to get out. It may be helpful to tell your therapist about your experience with creativity, but you should also feel free to keep it completely private.

With time and the creation of more images, meaning may begin to emerge. Particular symbols that give assurance or inspiration may recur. You may want to find a way to include these symbols in your life. One of my supervisors kept a large wooden turtle next to his chair. I don't know just what it meant to him, but he told me that it had been very helpful to him over the years.

For a guide to using art therapies see Kathy Malchiodi's *The Art Therapy Sourcebook*.[14]

Dreamwork

Both journaling and creative work can be applied to the exploration of dreams. Dreams often reveal the things we can't see or don't want to see. They seem to have served an evolutionary function,[15] nature's way of working through conflicts and anxiety by calling attention to what's been left out, including parts of our personality that we've otherwise been unaware of. We can tap into their ability to promote change more effectively if we approach them with consciousness.

While discussing your dreams with your therapist can be helpful, learning to work with them on your own will be an important skill to develop; you probably won't have time to cover them all in sessions, and being able to work with them on your own will also help you to continue your process once you leave therapy.

Try to record your dreams with a recording device or pad and pen as soon as you wake up. Dreams tend to break up once you begin to move; you may feel certain that you'll remember it, but they do fade quickly. Ideally you'll give yourself time and a quiet space to settle in to focus on your dream so you won't be disturbed. But if your time on your commute is all you have, that's better than not reflecting at all.

There are different approaches to using dreams, and I'll be able to give only a brief introduction to working with them. If you'd like other resources, two of the books that my clients have found most helpful are Sylvia Perera and Christopher Whitmont's *Dreams, A Portal to the Source*,[16] and Robert Johnson's *Inner Work*.[17] A more technical but very interesting book that compares seven different ways of interpreting a single dream is *Dream Interpretation: A Comparative Study*.[18] I don't recommend dream "cookbooks" with set interpretations. Engage with the dream personally, experientially, and emotionally; just "figuring out" what it means won't get you very far.

I'll demonstrate some general guidelines for using dreams for effective change with a short, relatively simple dream from a client named Tom, a successful writer. Here's the dream:

Mr. Spock from Star Trek has taken my cell phone.

- **Note the feeling.** Begin by noticing the feeling in the dream. Did it leave you anxious? Ecstatic?

○ *I was surprised when Spock took my phone—shocked, really. I thought he was on my side. But he was really obnoxious in the dream.*

- **Note the setting.** What is the setting of the dream? Is it your office, your childhood home, your bedroom? This may indicate symbolically what the dream is referring to.

  ○ *The dream started in my writing studio, but then Spock walked out into the living room with it and I followed him.*

- **Ask what part of yourself the characters represent.** The characters in the dream often represent different parts of your personality. How they appear in the dream will tell you something about that part of you.

  ○ *Spock represents the part of me that wants to be completely in control.*

- **Note your associations.** Write down your associations to all the elements of the dream. Do the setting, characters, objects, or action remind you of anything? What might they represent for you? If you can't come up with any personal associations to the characters or objects, imagine explaining them to someone from another galaxy. Consider day residue; what was happening the day before you had the dream? Are there any particular events that may have stirred things up that the dream might be referring to, such as a fight with your partner, or working on a creative project?

  ○ *Spock is all about self-control and being reasonable. I've always admired him, but sometimes he's missing something important.*

  ○ *My telephone is my way of staying connected with my friends. It hasn't been working very well, and it's running out of storage space. But without it I'd be up a creek. It holds all my important information.*

- **Put the story together.** Dreams use images to tell a story. Put all of the images together into a succinct narrative and see what story the dream is telling from a symbolic point of view. Take the dream seriously, but not literally.

- ○ *Someone, perhaps part of me, who likes to be reasonable and in control, isn't as nice as I thought he was. In fact he's taken my capacity to communicate with others, and my source of information. Even though that part (the phone) wasn't working very well, I'm still lost without it. This all starts happening in the place where I work, but then the action moves to where I socialize.*

- • *Is your therapist in there?* It may be particularly helpful to note if anyone in your dream reminds you of your therapist. What about your therapeutic process might it be bringing attention to? For example, does it imply that you're angry at your therapist, that you're idealizing her, or that the two of you are not on the same page?

  - ○ *My therapist has been challenging me to be more emotional in session. He says I'm holding a lot inside and there's no room left for me to hold it all in. I don't like the way he's challenging me, but I haven't been able to say anything to him.*

- • **Apply it to your current situation.** How does this relate to what you're going through in your life and in your work in therapy? What does it reveal to you that might be different from how you see things? What might the dream add to your understanding of yourself? Does it imply that doing something differently may be helpful?

  - ○ *Could something from my work life (my writing studio) be seeping over into my social life (the living room)? Am I too much like Spock? Is he taking away my ability to communicate, and my ability to access my own information? Or is he doing it because I need a new phone, a new way of communicating? Maybe he just seems obnoxious to me because he's challenging my defenses. Maybe he's like my therapist. Maybe I need to tell my therapist he's seemed obnoxious to me lately. Actually, come to think of it, he did suggest that I not answer or look at my cell phone in ses-sion. You know, maybe he could be a little more emotional himself instead of acting like Spock all the time.*

- **Paint, draw, or sculpt the character from the dream.** Bring it to life as vividly as possible. Give yourself time and space where you won't be disturbed. Choose a medium to depict the exchange between you and the characters and objects. What does it feel like to engage either one that way?
  - *I'm no good at art, but when I draw Spock, he seems really angular to me—very edgy—nothing smooth about him. What happens if I draw him with more curves? Hmmm, feels very different that way.*
- **Imagine what happens next.** Again, this will need quiet and privacy. In order to learn more about your inner world and to increase the impact of a dream, you can extend the drama of the dream onward using your imagination, as imagination often reveals contents of the unconscious. For instance, if your dream depicts you diving into the pond near your childhood home, what do you find there? If your dream portrays you leaving on an airplane, what happens on the ride and where does it take you? Yes—you *are* making it up. But why you make up one particular story rather than any other may help you understand what's happening unconsciously.
  - What happens next when you confront Spock and you don't have your cell phone?
    - *From here I won't try to replay Tom's experience word for word, but I will say that by extending the drama of the dream imagi-natively, he was able to gain insight into some of the questions that the dream had originally raised. But more importantly the experience of imagining began to change his feeling of all that Spock and the cell phone represented.*

- **Dialogue with a character from a dream.** Give yourself time and space where you won't be disturbed. Use your journal to record the conversation.
  - Bring to mind the character you dreamed of in as much detail as possible, reimagining the sights, the smells, the temperature, and anything else you can about the dream.
  - Ask the dream character whatever it is you would like to know about it, what it wants from you, or why it is the way it is. Be patient and give the dream character a chance to speak authentically. Don't give up if nothing happens right away.
  - Try not to let the ego prove what it wants to prove. Rather, be open to ways of seeing your situation that may be quite different from the way you usually do. Here again, any "results," such as a captivating dialogue, are less important than the experience of being open to the unconscious, the "other side."
  - You may not always like what you see immediately; the encounter with the unconscious sometimes reveals shadow, or as Bilbo Baggins found in *The Hobbit*, it may reveal the dragon that hides the treasure. Once you've finished the dialogue, give yourself time to slowly return to present time.
    - *Tom's dialogue with Spock helped him to answer the questions about whether Spock was part of himself or the therapist, and it turned out it was both in a way. Having a better sense of what problems that character caused him, what it wanted from him, what it had to offer him, increased Tom's flexibility, his ability to move from his working life to his "living room," his access to his own information, and his ability to communicate with others. He began to recognize when he got into "Spock mode," to use it when it was helpful but to push back against it when it was inappropriate. He was able*

to share, quite productively, some of his feelings about how I was working with him in session. And he upgraded his cell phone. Metaphorically.

Brent

One year after beginning therapy with me to work on his drinking, Brent was in a terrible car accident. The accident wasn't his fault, but his right arm was badly injured and he probably wasn't going to regain full use of it. One of Brent's favorite hobbies was riding his motorcycle, and we weren't sure if he'd be able to do that safely again. It left him feeling hopeless and powerless—feelings that he was not at all used to having. He had eight months of sobriety behind him, but he was tempted to drink again at this point. He had disgust for his damaged arm, and was starting to treat himself with contempt.

Then he had a dream that struck him: "I was walking down the road where the accident had happened. The same car that hit me comes barreling down the road. There's a dog—a husky—in the car's way. It's about to get hit. It doesn't see the car coming but I do. I have to decide quickly whether to push the dog out of the way or not. I lurch for it but it's too late. The car hits it and keeps going. Luckily it's only the front leg that gets hit, but he's definitely going to be lame now. Someone has to take care of the dog. I guess it's going to be me."

Brent is usually a bravado sort of guy, and nurturing wasn't his usual MO. But the image of the dog captivated him; he knew that there was something about the way he had been deriding himself and his injured arm that the dream was referring to.

Brent was very handy—he could fix anything—and he liked working with his hands. He had never done any sort of art, and had no ambitions to, but he did want to do something with this dog. With a combination of wood, wire, and string he constructed a life-sized model of the dog. Because his arm wasn't functional, it was a challenge to accomplish, but it was therapeutic on many levels. He started to develop ways to work with his functional arm and he felt good about that. He experimented with different versions of the dog: some with an injured leg, and some with the leg uninjured. He decided he liked the one with the injured leg better.

His feelings about his injury began to change; his bravado and macho found an object that needed him—his own injured body and soul. Making the dog helped him through the process of mourning. It was true that he wouldn't be able to do the things he could do before—but as he was changing through sobriety and our work together, there were things he could do. We talked about the feelings that he had had while he was building the dog at home—a combination of empathy, strength, and accomplishment. We also spoke about how this wasn't just about the injury to his arm, this was also about all the injuries that had happened before that made him more vulnerable to using alcohol to deal with feelings.

It wasn't an easy road for Brent. His injury required a great deal of physical and psychological adjustment that was particularly difficult as he was trying to maintain his sobriety. But through his work with the dream image he had something to hold onto that kept him stable enough—he had a responsibility to take care of himself.

SYMBOLIC ACTION: RITUAL AND CEREMONY

For thousands of years humans have used rituals to mark transitional milestones in their lives, times at which they wanted to begin living in a different way: child to adult, single to married, student to graduate, soldier to civilian, and lay to clergy. We've marked special occasions during which we adopt a different way of behaving, be it a spiritual retreat or a Mardi Gras celebration. These rituals have included physical actions that represented psychological change: making music, maintaining silence, reciting meaningful words, dancing, marching, wearing special clothing, eating special foods, fasting, calling friends and family together, going to a special place alone, and gesturing with the body to include it in the new way of living. The actions are all symbolic, but they are no less important or life-changing than the therapy homework assignments we have now. In fact, they may even be more effective.

According to Francesca Gino and Michael Norton,[19] behavioral scientists and professors at Harvard Business School, rituals can be extremely effective in alleviating grief, reducing anxiety, increasing confidence, and improving performance, and they can have a causal impact on people's thoughts, feelings, and behaviors. "What's more, rituals appear to benefit even people who claim not to believe that rituals work."

Yet today, the word "symbolic" usually carries with it the connotation of being "merely" symbolic, implying that anything symbolic is ineffectual. Even though many of our rituals today would appear to be designed more for show than psychological transformation, we still have the need for ritual to make these transitions.

If you want to make a specific change, designing and carrying out your own ceremony may help you to begin behaving differently. Your ceremony could be public—enlisting your community as witness can be very powerful—or private, which has the benefit of being easier to carry out and may leave you feeling freer to express yourself.

One woman who was entering a new stage of her life decided to burn all of her journals as a way of leaving her past behind. Others commit to a ritual of writing three pages in their journal every morning. Some mark their commitment to a marriage by placing a ring on their finger, while others mark a divorce by throwing the ring into the ocean. Some may stage a party with music and wild dancing to mark a change, while others mark it with quiet ceremonial chanting alone in their home. Some might choose to walk across the country, others might choose to kneel in their bedroom.

Taking action in a symbolic way impacts the unconscious in ways that logic can't. It serves as an energy transformer, releasing vitality by connecting with aspects of the unconscious that had been cut off previously. It sends a message to the entire psyche and body: the old story is finished and it's time to live the new story.

SUMMARY

1. Consider whether complementary practices such as exercise, meditation, or support groups might be helpful to you.
2. Decide what outer actions you need to take to apply your insights from sessions. What behavior will you need to change to reach your goals? Would specific assignments be helpful?
3. Develop intentions for more general goals.
4. Use journaling, creative expression, and your dreams to better understand and connect with yourself, and to develop your new narrative.
5. Consider having a ceremony, private or public, to symbolically mark the end of an old way of living, and the beginning of a new way.

Chapter Ten:

Into the Fire: Use Challenges as Opportunities for Growth

"I think I'm having pre-traumatic stress disorder."

"It is not light that we need, but fire; it is not the gentle shower, but thunder. We need the storm, the whirlwind, and the earthquake."
—Frederick Douglass

"What matters most is how well you walk through the fire."
—Charles Bukowski

Edward

Edward, the thirty-five-year-old account manager whom I described at the outset of this book, and who had questioned me about what it meant to "work on it in therapy," had come a long way. He had a better sense of the roots of his anger and a better way to handle it. He had made progress in being able to recognize and articulate other feelings.

He had also begun to realize that the situations that were the most difficult for him were also the ones that held the most opportunity for learning and change. Meetings with his boss in his "pressure cooker" office, for instance, had gone from being dreadful to being interesting. He began to look forward to them as material for our sessions and as opportunities to change his reactions.

But as he was starting to wind down and move toward ending therapy, two events threatened to derail his progress; he lost his biggest client at work, which meant his bonus would go down, and two days later he had to acknowledge what he had been trying to deny—his girlfriend had a serious cocaine problem that she wasn't willing to admit. That was a deal-breaker for him.

At first he was overwhelmed with anxiety and agitation, and simply needed to express all of his feelings in session. But soon it seemed that he was stuck in his reactions. I suggested that while these events were far more distressing than the meetings with his boss that we had worked on, perhaps we could see them in the same way: as "pressure cooker" opportunities, chances to go into the difficult places and handle them differently.

The loss of a girlfriend and a major client at the same time brought out feelings of anger at the injustice, and frustration at not being able to do anything, feelings to which he had overreacted in the past. Underneath were fears of being inadequate, vulnerable, and unloved. Noticing that he was in one of his challenging places and sensing the opportunities it presented gave Edward the feeling of getting out from under the problems, and getting on top of them, which helped him to regain his footing.

As far as the loss of his client went, even though there was no indication that he was at fault, he felt that the heat was on to get new clients, and it was a source of embarrassment for him. No one was saying that he had caused the loss of the account, but he still felt his status in the company was downgraded. To lose self-esteem at work at the same *time that his relationship was crashing was especially difficult. And as it turned out, his experience of the two was related.*

He had been with his girlfriend for two years. He found her attractive and enjoyed her warmth; she had brought emotion to his life in a way that had been lacking when he was single. Living without her was going to be hard: he was already feeling empty and worthless. But at the same time, he knew there was something he needed to learn from the situation. There was a pattern in his relationships with women and he didn't want to keep repeating it.

He realized that he presented himself as the heroic rescuer at first, and when he eventually brought his own needs and feelings into the relationship, the women he chose didn't like the more mundane Edward. This raised questions about himself: Why would he want to base a relationship on just one part of his personality? What was he trying to work out in these relationships?

Initially they made him feel good about himself, but the charismatic savior role was difficult to sustain. This also led Edward to question how he got his self-esteem; his efforts to get praise at work and from rescuing women weren't working for him. His unconscious purpose—to feel good about himself—was healthy and entirely human, but his technique— rescuing women and overachieving at work—wasn't working.

Edward extended his time in therapy to sort out these issues. Doing so allowed us to frame his handling of the two events as examples of how to handle difficult situations after he finished treatment: welcome adversity as an opportunity to learn about himself and to develop psychologically. He learned to put his struggles into a larger context: What did they mean in terms of the development of his personality? It would have been impossible for us to predict all of the problems he'd have to handle once he left treatment, but embracing this attitude prepared him to deal with them as effectively as he could.

Our tenth tool might be considered the master tool: master it and you'll find that the most difficult aspects of your life become less difficult. Using this tool will not completely spare you pain, but it will put the pain in a perspective that reduces the suffering it causes, and it will lead to the sort of change that you've sought in psychotherapy. Because this tool enlists all the other tools, and because it can change your outlook on the most challenging aspects of your life, I've saved it for last. Here it is:

To make the most effective use of psychotherapy, and to carry its benefits with you once you leave, welcome adversity and handle your difficulties as opportunities for change and growth: go into the fire with an expectation of positive change.

According to every major spiritual tradition, and according to an increasing amount of scientific research, adversity can be used as an opportunity for achieving transformation and well-being. This perspective is both profound and practical.

Consider this article by psychologist Mark Seery in the journal *Psychological Science*: "An Upside to Adversity?: Moderate Cumulative Lifetime Adversity Is Associated with Resilient Responses in the Face of Controlled Stressors."[1] Seery's own research and his review of similar research indicate that experiencing a moderate amount of adversity, as opposed to no adversity or frequent adversity, is associated with optimal well-being: lower global distress, lower negative responses to pain, less functional impairment (from, for instance, back pain), fewer post-traumatic symptoms, and greater life satisfaction.

Seery and his colleagues conclude that optimal adversity leads to resilience; too much adversity and you fry your neural system and get sick, too little adversity and you have no resilience. Psychologist Louis Cozolino explains that "mild to moderate stress activates neural growth hormones supportive of new learning."[2] Psychological research is bearing out what we've known intuitively for a long time; a certain amount of adversity fosters strength. If stress is within an ideal range it is adaptive.

But what's optimal? How much fire is good for us? What's optimal is determined not just by any objective measure of the stress we experience, or how threatening it is in light of our material resources; it's also determined by the way we respond to the stress and the meaning we attribute to it. The more you freak out, and the longer you freak out, the more of the stress hormone cortisol you pump throughout your body, and the more wear and tear that it takes on body and soul. Your attitude toward that stress, how you react to going into the fire, partially determines whether it leads to resilience or to a cascade of destructive hormones.

So, if you see a stressful event coming and say, "Here comes the fire. This may hurt, but I'll come out better on the other side," rather than, "Oh no, I'm doomed," you're more likely to build resilience and well-being rather than dig a deeper rut of anxiety, depression, and ill-health.

But since it's easier to preach this tool than to practice it, I'll explain the why and how of this tool from a few different angles. First I'll describe the perspective that wisdom traditions have conveyed through their images and rituals for thousands of years. Then I'll look at some of the scientific research about post-traumatic growth. I'll discuss how to use therapy to develop this perspective and some of the limitations and dangers of it. Finally, I'll explain that some of the challenges we encounter are indications that our constructive unconscious is trying to change how we're living. Growth is the natural inclination of the human psyche for the entire life span, but growth entails challenge. Learning to read these signs may be the summit of your work in therapy.

MYTHOLOGICAL AND SPIRITUAL PERSPECTIVES ON CHALLENGES

Religion and mythology have long recognized that our attitude toward difficulties and our response to them impacts our quality of life. For millennia they've used rituals and images to help us to prepare to respond to stress in a way that promotes growth. Many wisdom traditions use images of going into a fire and emerging transformed so that the person comes to welcome the fire as sacred, creating a very different attitude toward tribulations.

From the ritual of walking on coals practiced by many cultures, to the Celtic celebration of Beltane ("Bright Fire"), in which participants jump over fires and dance around them to heal, purify, and ensure fertility; from Pentecost, in which flames light on the heads of the Disciples, to Shiva dancing in a ring of fire; from alchemists using heat to turn lead into gold, to the image of the phoenix arising from the fire in rebirth. From lighting a candle to building a bonfire, spiritual traditions have prepared their participants symbolically to handle the rough stuff, both before and after it occurs.

The wisdom of these traditions is that challenges, often symbolized by fire, create situations in which we become more malleable and open to transformation. Like metal forged in the fire, once we come through it, we're stronger and more adaptive. The fire also purifies: it can burn away the old narrative and open the possibility of creating a new one.

As Joseph Campbell points out,[3] the hero or heroine is always faced with trials. These are obstacles to be gotten past, animals to be conquered or befriended, objects to be retrieved, rivers to be crossed, mountains to be scaled, and hells to be descended into. No trial, no hero. Our everyday trials are not always so obvious, but they're just as important. And anyone who works on it in therapy is a hero or heroine.

Those of you who are spiritually oriented may *find* the meaning and opportunity in situations that were created for you; you may have a clear sense that providence is leading you into particular opportunities for growth. Some of you may find synchronicity in the challenges of your life, a sense that the supposed coincidences actually have meaning in terms of your spiritual development. This type of faith has great psychological advantages, including a sense of calm under pressure, lowered anxiety, and a sense of meaning in what you experience. Spirituality is a strong predictor of post-traumatic growth.[4]

THE SCIENTIFIC PERSPECTIVE: POST-TRAUMATIC GROWTH RESEARCH

But those of you who embrace a more secular or humanistic perspective might not *find* intrinsic, pre-ordained meaning in situations, rather you may see them as opportunities to *make* occasions for growth; you may decide to *choose* to turn difficulties into opportunities.

Consider some of the possible benefits that research identifies as results of post-traumatic growth:

- Enhanced social resources such as better relationships with friends
- Enhanced personal resources such as better self-concept
- New or improved coping skills such as better problem-solving abilities[5]
- Greater appreciation of life and a changed sense of priorities
- Realizations of new possibilities and paths for one's life.[6]

Challenge and crisis can help forge personalities that are resilient, strong, and flexible. But whether this happens depends to some extent on the attitude of the individual both before and after the event.

The more open to experience and emotions we are, the more likely it is that we will grow as the result of difficulties and crises.[7] "Oh no!" closes us down and prevents positive change, whereas, "What can I learn from this?" opens us up and allows for the possibility of growth.

One of the most prominent researchers in the field of post-traumatic growth, Richard Tedeschi, points out, "Growth, however, does not occur as a direct result of trauma. It is the individual's struggle with the new reality in the aftermath of trauma that is crucial in determining the effect to which post-traumatic growth occurs."[8] Tedeschi's team has found that "cognitive reprocessing," deliberate thinking about the event after it's happened, correlates with post-traumatic growth. This reworking helps to challenge an old narrative and create a new one. How we interpret and understand what we've been through will partially determine our mental health afterward.[9]

It would be understandable if any of you were thinking, "But how could anyone possibly find growth in something that's really horrendous?" There are limits and cautions to this approach, which I'll discuss below. But remarkably, the greater the degree of stress (the hotter the fire), the greater the potential degree of growth.[10]

This isn't to say that some people don't completely crash after trauma and other challenges. Many do. And that's part of what I'm trying to prevent with this tool.

JILL TAYLOR

Consider as an example Jill Taylor, a Harvard-trained brain scientist who experienced a stroke in the left hemisphere of her brain when she was thirty-seven. As a result of that experience she wrote a book called *My Stroke of Insight*. While most people would consider a stroke like this a disaster, she experienced it as a release from a stressful way of living, and as an opportunity to start living from both sides of her brain:

"My stroke of insight is that at the core of my right hemisphere consciousness is a character that is directly connected to my feeling of deep inner peace, it is completely committed to the expression of peace, love, joy, and compassion in the world."[11]

She experienced both a burning off of the extraneous wiring that had kept her compulsively operating out of her left brain, and a rising up of a part of her personality that had been sequestered before. She started living more in the right side of her brain. And she has *made* incredible meaning of her experience. She lectures throughout the world about what she has learned through it. She doesn't say that she believes that this was meant to happen. But she has *created* meaning out of it.

Knowing in advance that these opportunities can advance your psychological development makes challenging experiences less destructive and potentially *con*structive. My goal in this chapter is to help you use this tool to process difficulties once they arise, but—and perhaps more importantly—to also help you look forward; if you can see upcoming difficulties as opportunities to build resilience and character, you're more likely to be able to use them effectively.

And they become a lot less daunting. Instead of waiting until after the difficult event, you can see it coming with curiosity rather than dread. While some of you may already have the openness to experience and feeling and the optimistic attitude that's helpful in this, with intention and persistence anyone can develop it. The mind can change the brain.

Trauma shatters the old narrative—for better or worse. The old building comes down in a fire—and offers the possibility of a new one rising on the same site. This isn't just abstract—it literally shakes up our old neural structures and offers the possibility of laying down new neural pathways. And writing a new story.

DANGERS AND LIMITS TO USING THE FIRE

It's seventh grade and I'm walking to school with my best friend Eddie. I'm telling him about this idea that what doesn't kill you just makes you stronger. Eddie is interested in science so he spontaneously decides to conduct an experiment—without the prior approval of the subject, I might add. He takes the opportunity to punch me in the arm. And Eddie is no weakling. "So, do you feel stronger now?" he asks me. So much for that idea. But it did make me wiser. What doesn't kill us can inflict damage and doesn't always make us stronger. Fire can also burn painfully and destructively. So let's also be aware of the dangers of going into the fire.

People with certain personality styles, the martyr or sacrificial victim for instance, could take this to heart a little too much and use it to justify subjecting themselves to too much fire: "It's OK, I can handle that committee, too. It builds character." Yes, and it could also lead to burnout. You may find yourself getting into the drama of the fire—always needing to have something wrong—and either looking for things that have gone wrong, or even creating them. It can become a bad habit. This could manifest in taking on too many responsibilities, or taking on the worst ones.

The idea of using challenges could also be inflating and make the ego feel that it can do things it really can't. At times we may feel that we should be able to handle the fire, no matter how hot or how long we're in it. We need to be able to get out of the fire periodically. Sweat lodge ceremonies are usually broken into four rounds; the participants douse themselves with water or roll in the snow to cool off between rounds. We all need breaks from the fire.

The stories of heroes and heroines have evolved and survived because they serve as models about how to live our lives, about how to go into the fire and how to use it. But that can create another problem: an overidentification with the archetype of the hero. For some who have a propensity for risky behavior, this could be like the moth being drawn to the flame. Or like playing with fire.

Some of you might be tempted to use this tool to avoid the feelings that come up in difficult situations. For instance, if you lose a friend or an opportunity, before rushing on to the bright side of the loss (I'll have more time to pursue other things, or this will help me to understand what my clients go through, or I needed to learn to be more independent anyway), let yourself mourn what you've lost. Otherwise you risk engaging in a spiritual bypass—focusing on a psychological or spiritual benefit that would appear to be lofty and positive, but avoiding difficult feelings that are important to go through, rather than around.

But perhaps the most dangerous possibility of this attitude is that it may be going too far to ask someone who has experienced tragedy to find meaning in it or make meaning from it. We need to be realistic about when we can adopt this perspective. Some situations are so horrific that asking someone to see what he or she can learn from the event would be insensitive, inappropriate, and possibly destructive. If you aren't able to find or make meaning out of your experience, please don't feel that you should.

EVERYDAY ALCHEMY: USING ADVERSITY IN PSYCHOTHERAPY

The capacity to use adversity for healing and growth arises naturally while we're in psychotherapy. You might not even be aware of it developing as you watch for the difficult events that are most helpful to talk about, and learn from them each week in session. But whether this perspective develops automatically or intentionally, you'll want to bring conscious attention to it so that you can use it at will both while you're in treatment and once you've stopped attending sessions.

The challenges and adversity I'm referring to run the gamut from minor everyday annoyances to the brutalities of trauma. We can use the small trials to build the ability to handle the larger ones. Setting intentions in advance to use hardship helps us to cope with the small problems; the larger ones usually confront us unexpectedly. As the research on adversity and resilience demonstrates, the skill we build handling the smaller challenges—using the mild fires for growth— helps us to handle the big fires. Seeing the value in the little challenges that we bring to our sessions helps us to build the resilience that helps us to deal with the challenges that will inevitably come later. I call this everyday alchemy—we turn lead into gold. But it doesn't happen magically; it happens with perspective and effort.

169

Many of us are forced into therapy by challenges that feel insurmountable. And many of us complete therapy in much better shape overall because we used those original issues as opportunities for healing and growth in more ways than we had expected.

The emotional challenges we face have two aspects: the primary emotion and the secondary emotion. The primary emotion, such as anger, sadness, or anxiety, is usually an expectable human reaction and hurts enough in itself. But we often add another layer, a secondary reaction ("Oh NO!") to the original one, which makes it worse. Next thing you know your shoulders are scrunched up, your head is tucked in and down, your jaw is clenched, and you're pumping out cortisol like crazy and suppressing your immune system. Viewing the original problem as an opportunity rather than as a disaster helps to prevent this secondary emotion from becoming an additional problem. Each session we attend offers the possibility of adopting and exercising this attitude.

Rather than respond to difficulties by becoming tense, saying, "Oh no, not that again," and drawing back, you can instead become curious about your problems and welcome the chance to respond differently: "Oh, here's that situation we were talking about the other day. God, it feels awful, but maybe I don't have to respond the way I used to. That felt even worse! What happens if I respond differently?" It will take some exercise in therapy to get you to the point where you can embrace this attitude and welcome challenges, but with time you can see these experiences of going "into the fire" as opportunities for transformation.

So, for instance, if you tell yourself that you're "going through a break*down*," you may make the problem worse. However, if you understand the difficult situation as a possible break*through,* a rite of passage, with all its implications for progress, that perspective removes the judgment and panic and infuses energy and curiosity.

In Chapter Four I discussed the tool of speaking openly with your therapist about subjects that may not feel comfortable at first. These interactions can serve as practice sessions for the bigger world.

Like rituals of going into the fire, your sessions provide opportunities to have intense experiences that transform you and help to develop a positive attitude about challenges. There may well be issues in your relationship with your therapist that present these opportunities: feeling judged by your therapist or feeling judgmental of her, feeling like you're failing as a patient or feeling that your therapist is failing you.

In fact psychotherapy has been referred to as "The Successful Failure," because inevitably your therapist will fail you in some way—probably a small way—but one that's important to you. Then you may experience your fire, the place that feels disturbing. Navigating this failure can be curative. What had seemed inevitably debilitating before becomes not only tolerable, but therapeutic.

Use the Problem as the Antidote

"The impediment to action advances action. What stands in the way is the way."

—Marcus Aurelius

When we choose to use a problem constructively it's similar to what Buddhists call using the problem as the antidote.

Once upon a time a Buddhist teacher was going into dangerous territory where there were scores of dangerous bandits. His followers pleaded with him not to go there. "You're gonna get *killed*," they told him. But he insisted on going anyway, and of course the bandits surrounded him and threatened to kill him.

So he tells the bandits, "I'll pay you some money now to be my bodyguard, and once we complete our journey safely I'll pay you more. And if you take good care of us, we'll recommend you to safeguard more people. This way you get more money, you can have a family, you can stop living in cold caves, and no one gets hurt!" By enlisting the bandits as his protectors, he took the energy that everyone said was dangerous, and enlisted it in his own protection.

As the Body Heals and Grows, So Does the Mind

The mind operates in similar fashion to the body in many ways, and there is a biological parallel to what I am suggesting: physical exercise. When you exercise to the point where you're really pushing yourself—for example, running as opposed to jogging—and your heart rate goes up to 75 to 90 percent of its maximum capacity, your body goes into a state of emergency. Your muscles can't get enough oxygen, and so instead of burning just oxygen, they burn creatine, releasing energy. Then you can "feel the burn." Runners sometimes refer to this as thigh burn. You're actually breaking down muscle so that it builds up again more strongly.[12]

I experienced this when I was a professional trumpet player. There were certain exercises I would play to deliberately push my embouchure to the point of muscle failure, and the creation of new muscle. This eventually helped me to play high notes and to play long, demanding concerts.

When you exercise any muscle this intensely, you produce Human Growth Hormone (HGH), which helps you to stay young. Without exercise, we produce less and less HGH as we get older. But with it, we create more muscle and burn more fat and carbohydrates. We also increase neuronal growth. So when you're pushing yourself and challenging yourself your body goes into a mild state of emergency. You go into the fire. And that's when you get the most benefit from physical exercise.

To translate this into psychological exercise we don't need to create problems; we need only to see and handle the ones we have differently. Your therapist's office becomes a bit like a gym. Experience and use the fire there consciously as a "Psychological Human Growth Hormone" to create psychological strength.

Therapy ideally creates a context of safety and calm into which we can bring our stress, and experience it without adding an extra layer of *dis*tress or an extra dollop of cortisol, but rather with an attitude of welcome. If you can develop this attitude more consciously, and have it as a tool at your disposal when things are looking grim, the impact of crises will be less negative and quite possibly even positive.

USING THE FIRE

But however great the rewards of going into your own fire consciously, it's not so easy to do. So here are some suggestions for using the challenges that you run into for your psychological transformation:

Know your fires: Identify the particular places that you can expect to be challenged. All the tools we've discussed prepare you for this; you may experience the fire when you become afraid and exclude certain parts of your personality; you may experience it when you're tempted to shut down and stop expressing yourself; you may experience it when you feel defensive and are tempted to blow up and blame others; you may feel it when you want to attack yourself rather than be curious; you may experience it when you feel tempted to live out a rescue fantasy.

Use the body: Memorize what it feels like in your body when you begin to overreact to the fire. Does it lean forward? Tense up? Become shaky? Then, once you know that feeling, develop a method such as deep breathing to release physical tension. Practice it as often as you need to when your body clinches in reaction to challenges. Relaxing the body can relax the mind.

Have your new story at hand: Having a sense of your intentions and your new narrative will also help you to recognize when you're in the fire and to use it for positive change. This is the time to replace the old story with the new story. If, for instance, you have an interview, audition, or any other situation where you will be evaluated, know in advance that this could bring up feelings of inadequacy. Change the agenda from succeeding on the outside to succeeding on the inside by remaining aware of your fear of inadequacy and not buying into it. Replace the sense of inadequacy with a realistic sense of your strengths.

Use fire as a cue for curiosity: When you get to the fire, get curious about what it may be communicating about what's happening inside rather than what's happening outside. For instance, if social anxiety is one of your fires, what is the anxiety saying? This can help you to not become anxious about being anxious—which would otherwise be a recipe for a panic attack. Instead, you say, "OK, here it is again. Now, where do I feel it in my body? How intense is it this time? What might it be telling me?"

Name the fire and use an image: Once you're in the fire you need to recognize it. "This is it. This is the fire that I knew would come and here's the opportunity to try out a new way of responding." If the image of fire doesn't work for you, choose another image that serves as a reminder of your intentions. It will help you to act—to *do something!*—rather than react. The important thing is to see that it's part of a larger process that could well move you forward. Change happens in the here and now. The tendency is to wait for all the stars to be in alignment before you can work on it, when everything is easier and calmer. But the best time to change is when you're in the fire, when you're most pliable and most transformable.

Welcome the fire—don't put it out: You can't cook without heat. If we don't recognize that we're in the fire, and what it's for, we may become afraid and try to put out the fire prematurely with any of the many forms of avoidance that are available to us.

Here's an ancient story that demonstrates what might be lost:

The Fire Refused: Demeter Tries to Make an Immortal

Demeter was the Greek Mother-Goddess, the one the Greeks would look to for higher hopes in this life and the afterlife. When her daughter Persephone is abducted by the god of the Underworld,

Hades, Demeter is completely distraught, and stops everything from growing on the earth. She wanders far and wide looking for Persephone. She takes the form of an old woman and finds shelter with a family in their home. In exchange for their hospitality, she wants to give the family a gift; she decides to make the baby immortal by secretly putting it into the fire, a standard technique among the gods. She begins to do this each night when the others have gone to bed. But one night the mother of the child walks in during the treatment and screams bloody murder. Demeter gives up, takes the child out of the fire, and it doesn't get to be immortal.

The next time you're in the fire, consider, "This could be Demeter putting me here."

WORK WITH THE CONSTRUCTIVE UNCONSCIOUS, YOUR INNATE DRIVE TOWARD PSYCHOLOGICAL WELL-BEING

Here's one more reason to see the fire as an opportunity: you may be trying to work something out through your challenges without knowing it. Psychological and emotional struggles may indicate that you've been unconsciously trying to heal, grow, or master a difficult issue, but that that original intent has been blocked and its energies have become pressured and misdirected. If you can find the original intent and pursue it consciously, you may be able to resolve the emotional distress that the blockage caused, and achieve the progress that you were aiming for in the first place.

This perspective is at the very core of what many of us therapists believe to be a central goal of therapy: forming a deep, healthy, and informative connection between your conscious ego and your constructive unconscious. Consciousness and a functioning ego are indispensable to healthy living, but so is cooperation with what's going on beneath the surface in the unconscious. Having the two working together is what will help you continue to remain healthy and grow after your sessions are over.

SAMANTHA

Samantha had been a political science professor for twenty-five years. She took great pride in her self-reliance and self-control, and had entered therapy quite reluctantly only after acknowledging to herself and her doctor that she was abusing prescription medications. She had had a skiing injury for which pain medication had been prescribed, but, as she described it, she became a little too fond of it. Once we began meeting she enlisted her self-discipline and was able to stop using the pills.

But then she had to face a depression she had been trying to avoid since long before her injury. The story Samantha told herself for most of her life was that she did not need to introspect; she felt she didn't need to pay attention to what was going on inside of her. Anyone who was strong put his or her attention out in the world where it belonged. And in regard to depression, she had told herself, "Strong people don't get depressed."

But by this point her story had changed. When we started to explore what the depression was about she just shrugged her shoulders, and in a moment of unusual spontaneity said, "Well, shouldn't we all be depressed about what's going on in the world? Isn't it futile? Isn't the rational thing to do to just give up?"

On one level I could have agreed with Samantha. I shared her concern about the many grave problems in our world, but the response still didn't make sense for a woman who'd been an activist most of her life. So I questioned her: "Do you really want to give up on the world? It's completely contrary to everything that you tell me you've stood for in your life. Could it be that there's something else that you really need to give up on?"

My question didn't bring her immediately to an "aha" moment, but it did engage her curiosity over a period of many months during which she explored the theme of "giving up." An extremely disciplined woman, Samantha had never included the phrase "giving up" in her vocabulary. But she recalled many passing fantasies of just falling down and being put to bed rest for months, fantasies of getting drunk and shouting at the top of her lungs, and fantasies of turning off her constant thinking about the world and just not caring so much. None of which had she entertained for more than a moment.

But all of these fantasies indicated that another part of her was trying to get something across: that her ego had taken over too much control and she needed to give some of it up. Her depression, and even her use of medication, had been an unconscious attempt to give up on something, to let go of her attempt to control everyone and everything around her. Her conscious side said, "Control is the rational way to approach life," but her unconscious side was saying, "You need to give up this control."

It seemed that because she wasn't paying attention to what was happening inside, her unconscious, in an attempt to compensate the ego's overly dominant role, had withdrawn her energy in an effort to force her to let go. In effect it forced her to give up, but it happened in an exaggerated way that was neither conscious nor effective. When energy is withdrawn this way, it can lead to depression.

Learning to listen to that other side—the part of the psyche I call the constructive unconscious—and work in cooperation with it became a guiding theme in our work. It also brought meaning to her challenges and helped her to weather them with less suffering. She eventually returned to her activism, balancing it with an appreciation for what was happening inside of her.

The unconscious has its own wisdom and its own goals that we ideally work with, rather than against. When the constructive goals of the unconscious are blocked, we often end up in the fire. Learning what the original intent was helps us to get through the fire and come out more whole on the other side.

Here's another example:

An eight-year-old girl is having trouble in school. The teachers think she has a learning disorder; she can't sit still or concentrate.

She's disturbing other kids and they can't teach her. So they send her to a specialist.

The specialist speaks to the girl for a while and then tells her, "I need to talk to your mother. If you'd please, wait here for a few moments." He turns the radio on as he leaves. He and the mother watch what happens; she ecstatically breaks into full-throttle dance all over the office. The doctor tells the mother, "Your daughter isn't sick; she's a dancer. Take her to a dance school."

This is the story of Gillian Lynne, who went on to dance as a soloist with London's Royal Ballet and to choreograph musicals such as *Cats* and *Phantom of the Opera*. The specialist simply looked to see where her supposedly pathological energy wanted to go. He understood what her fire was for.

TEMPERATURE'S RISING

Again, the mind and the body operate in similar fashion. When we have a fever, our elevated temperature sets into motion a number of bodily functions that increase our immunity and our ability to fight off infection. While a fever above 102 degrees may become dangerous, temperatures lower than that usually serve a healthy function. Sometimes patients worry about fever, when fever is actually only an indication that we're working on something that's happening out of sight. Similarly, the constructive unconscious may raise our emotional temperature to fight off an imbalance and to deal with a psychological problem that's not so obvious.

But just as with a fever, if the emotional signal gets too hot, the healthy motivation has gone awry, and could become destructive. It needs conscious correction. Just because the unconscious is trying to work something out, doesn't mean that it will succeed on its own. Environmental problems such as early neglect and trauma, and the fears that result from them, often lead to protective strategies that keep our natural, healthy inclinations from accomplishing their ends.

LOOK FOR THE HEALTHY INTENT

When you experience psychological challenges and your emotional temperature is rising, look carefully to see if you're blocking any motivations of the constructive unconscious. Here are some examples:

- As in Samantha's situation, depression may signify a forceful attempt from the unconscious to make us turn inward and adjust our priorities, such as not taking too much responsibility.
- Restless anxiety can be an indication that action needs to be taken, perhaps leading to more engagement with others and the outer world.
- Anger that won't go away may point toward an old, frozen need to stand up to something that happened long ago, indicating that we're holding onto anger because we still feel that we need to protect ourselves.
- If there is a part of your personality—vulnerable, strong, or mischievous, for example—that keeps popping out when you least want it to, it may indicate that that part of the personality may be trying to force its way toward inclusion into consciousness, but your inhibitions force it to do so in an exaggerated way.
- If you find yourself compulsively cleaning or working, ask whether there might be some sort of mastery you're trying to achieve, mastery of your own instincts or mastery over what you experience as a hostile environment.
- If you notice that you keep ending up with problematic partners, ask what old relationship you're trying to rework, or, what is it about the people you're drawn to that you're trying unconsciously to integrate.

I'm not suggesting that these symptoms always mean the same thing, but rather that the original healthy intent in any of these cases may become distorted or exaggerated, and that if we understand the original motivation of the constructive unconscious we can work with it rather than against it. I am suggesting that we ask not only why we have certain challenges, but *what do we have these challenges for? Where might they lead us?*

ALLY WITH THE CONSTRUCTIVE UNCONSCIOUS

As I suggested in Chapter Three, our unconscious motivations are not all destructive. In fact they are basically constructive, but the protective strategies we developed as a result of our injuries, frailties, and environments often get in the way of our using these motivations effectively.

These situations present challenges that carry meaning and possibility. Learning to be attuned to your drive toward well-being will help you to manage and thrive when you experience difficulties. Adopting this attitude creates a relationship with your own psyche that forms the foundation for a healthy and meaningful life. It also creates a shift from thinking pathologically—in terms of disease—to thinking in terms of well-being. Understanding the healing, development, or mastery you've been trying unconsciously to achieve, and having consciousness cooperate with the constructive unconscious to achieve these goals, might be considered the most important goal that you can accomplish in psychotherapy. It may take longer to achieve than simply eradicating symptoms, but in the long run it's more effective, and perhaps more importantly, it's far more rewarding.

SUMMARY

1. Choose the most difficult events of your week to talk about in your session.
2. Develop an attitude in which you see challenges as opportunities for change.

3. Try to find or make meaning from the challenges you face—before, during, and after the time you experience them.

4. Choose an image such as fire to help you label the situations that will offer opportunities for change.

5. Recognize when you are "in the fire," in your most challenging situations.

6. Consider that your challenges may be the result of blocked efforts to grow and move toward wholeness. Try to understand what the constructive unconscious is trying to achieve and work with it consciously to attain a more balanced state.

Afterword

THE SEVEN DWARFS AFTER THERAPY

What does it mean to get the "most" out of psychotherapy? The "most" may be a lot more than you originally thought: Many people have little idea of the possibilities it offers. In addition to removing symptoms and healing wounds, therapy can also help us to develop our authentic personality, forge better relationships, and find more direction and meaning in life. Or put differently, therapy offers us the possibility of wholeness: not just a better-functioning personality, but a larger and more fulfilling one, rather than a limited identity such as Grumpy, Sleepy, Bashful, Sneezy, Dopey, or even Happy.

This is a lot to do. In explaining what it means to "work on it" in therapy, I've handed you ten tools to learn and then asked you to do five or six tasks with each of them. But we all have the potential capacity to use these tools, even if some of them are unfamiliar at first. And you don't need to use them all at once. As a hero or heroine on a journey, you'll learn to use a compass first, a rope later, a shield after that, and flint and stone later still. Afterward you'll always have these skills at your disposal.

I hope that my underlying philosophy has become clear: psychotherapy works with the natural tendencies of the human psyche to grow and heal as we develop as individuals. But because it's often a nasty world out there, and because we're complex, imperfect creatures, we often get thrown off of our natural course.

Perhaps it's not fair that we should have to go to all this work just to get back on course, but perhaps it's the getting off and on course that really makes us uniquely, wonderfully, and beautifully human, and that makes each of us capable of playing his or her own individual role in the larger drama. For while we may retreat into sessions for a short time each week, this is only preparation for an advance into the greater world of creativity, relationships, family, and community. May your work lead you to a richer and more fulfilling life.

Appendix A: *In the Beginning:* Starting Therapy

WHERE TO LOOK

Searching for the right therapist can incite many feelings, including excitement, frustration, hope, and discouragement. But take heart. There are plenty of good therapists out there, and one of them is going to be yours.

Start by asking friends, family, clergy, physicians, college psychology or social work departments, or employee assistance programs for recommendations. While it is best to get a suggestion from someone who knows the therapist firsthand, it's not a good idea to share a therapist with a friend or a family member. You'll want to feel completely free to express yourself, and sharing a therapist can lead to a subtle but limiting reluctance to say everything you need to say. Nor is it a good idea to work with a therapist whom you know or run into in your social or professional life. That can get very messy.

If you can't get a referral from someone you know, or if you prefer to keep your search private, turn directly to the Internet and search for "psychotherapist" and the name of your town.

If you plan to work with a therapist who is on your insurance plan, start with a list of therapists (usually listed as psychologists, social workers, or psychiatrists) who participate in your network. Many therapists do not participate, so you'll save yourself time by going to that list directly.

It's usually best to choose a therapist who is licensed to practice as a psychologist, social worker, psychoanalyst, psychiatrist, family therapist, mental health counselor, or psychiatric nurse practitioner. The term "psychotherapist" means nothing in terms of training or licensing. Most states require a license to practice in the field of mental health, but some do not. It's possible for anyone to call himself a psychotherapist and have had no training or accreditation at all. So, while a license does not guarantee that a therapist is competent and ethical, it does increase the likelihood that he or she is.

Your therapist should have at least a master's degree in her field. If the work described in this book appeals to you, you'll ideally choose someone who has completed postgraduate training in psychodynamic psychotherapy or psychoanalysis.

More years of experience are usually a good indication of more skill, knowledge, and proficiency. But professional status, positions of authority, and publications don't necessarily indicate that someone is a good psychotherapist or a good fit for you. And beware of therapists who promise too much too quickly.

I would also strongly suggest that you choose a therapist who has been in therapy herself. It's OK to ask if she has been. Be wary of therapists who aren't willing to undergo the same thing they expect you to go through, and of therapists who feel that they don't need therapy. Going to therapy is essential training to becoming a therapist.

WHAT TYPE OF THERAPY TO CHOOSE

The tools that I've described are effective in the many types of therapy that come under the general heading of traditional talk therapy, or psychodynamic psychotherapy. These include psychoanalytic psychotherapy, depth psychotherapy, insight-oriented psychotherapy, expressive therapy, and most forms of psychoanalysis including Jungian, Freudian, object relations, self-psychology, interpersonal, and relational analysis.

Newer forms of short-term therapy such as Cognitive Behavioral Therapy (CBT) and Dialectical Behavior Therapy (DBT), which tend to be far more structured, use some, but not all of these tools. They tend to target specific symptoms or focus on the development of coping skills, rather than overall personality development. If your goal is simply to stop having panic attacks, eradicate a particular phobia, or get out of a mild depression, shorter therapies such as these may be adequate to address the symptoms.

We know that different types of therapy tend to be just as effective[1] in terms of symptom removal when dealing with limited and straightforward issues. But for broader, more complex and less specifically defined issues such as personality and relation-ship issues, psychodynamic psychotherapy is usually more effective. (See Appendix C for more about this.)

You can ask potential therapists what sort of therapy they practice, but more importantly, ask how they see therapy working for you. Many therapists are eclectic, and whether they practice a particular form of therapy may be less important than an under-standing between the two of you of what it will take for you to get better. If they can explain how they work in terms that make sense to you, that's more helpful than any label. You should feel free to shop around and interview a few therapists before making your decision.

THE CONSULTATION

Many people contact prospective therapists by email these days. This may be the most comfortable medium if you don't like speaking on the phone, but you can tell a lot more about them from even a brief phone conversation. Most therapists are willing to spend a few minutes with you on the phone to make sure that it makes sense for the two of you to meet for a consultation. Take advantage of that and listen to any feelings you have in reaction to them. A phone conversation may be adequate to rule out a therapist, but it's not adequate to rule one in. Before you commit to work with someone be sure to have at least one consultation session with him or her in person.

A consultation session is an initial meeting with a therapist in which the two of you discuss your needs and get a feel for whether the fit between the two of you is a good one. You may decide to have two or even three consultations with the therapist if you aren't certain after the first session whether he or she is a good fit for you. Also, don't feel that you need to commit to the therapist in the consultation. You can go home and reflect on it or sleep on it. It's an important decision and deserves reflection.

In the consultation, the therapist will want to know what issues you want to work on and perhaps something about your background. This is an exploratory session. Don't expect to understand the source of your problems, or have them solved in your first meeting. But do watch to see if you feel comfortable with the therapist, that she listens well, and that she understands what your goals are.

You'll probably find that the meeting goes by very quickly. If you have questions for the therapist, such as issues of confidentiality, or her training and her experience, it may be a good idea to write them down before you go into your session. Be sure to find out what the therapist's cancellation and payment policies are.

Find out if she has time to see you on a regular basis. If you choose to work together, you should have a specific time (or two) each week that you know is set aside for you. This time should be one that you can realistically attend each week. Getting the most out of therapy will require that you attend your sessions consistently: missing sessions makes it hard to follow the themes you discover, and hard to follow up on the issues that you spoke about in your last session. Skipping sessions dilutes the efficacy of your work.

PAYING

The cost of therapy is significant and also needs to be dealt with realistically. Before you begin calling therapists, decide whether you'll use your insurance or pay out of pocket. If you plan to use insurance find out from your carrier in advance whether you need a referral, whether you have out-of-network benefits, if you have a deductible, what percentage of the fee your insurance covers, and how many sessions are covered. If you plan to use your insurance but don't have out-of-network benefits, you'll need to find someone in your network. You can get a list of in-network providers from your carrier.

If you plan to pay out of pocket, decide what you can afford to pay on a weekly basis. Some therapists are willing to use a sliding scale and lower their fee if you can't afford their full fee, but this doesn't necessarily mean they'll accept whatever fee you have in mind. Some therapists prefer to meet with a prospective client before they agree to a reduced fee in order to get an accurate sense of what their resources are. The fee should be an honest reflection of what you are able to pay, but it should also be sustainable; it shouldn't cause you too much stress or lead to a premature ending of the therapy.

If you can't afford to pay out of pocket, or if your insurance won't pay enough for you to manage the rest of the fee, you may want to consider seeing a therapist at a clinic or a training institute. Most large cities have psychoanalytic training institutes at which the students already have some education and experience in doing psychotherapy, but are engaging in postgraduate training to improve their skills. These institutes provide depth therapy at a reduced fee. To find one, simply search the Internet for "psychoanalytic training institute" and the name of your city.

You may also consider going to a public clinic or hospital. These have some disadvantages; therapists don't always stay as long at their positions in clinics and hospitals as they do in private practice, and some clients feel less comfortable with the arrangements of public settings. But clinics do have the advantage of reduced fees and other resources, such as psychiatrists on staff for medications, and, in some clinics, therapeutic groups that can supplement your individual work.

THE DECISION

You could drive yourself crazy trying to find the perfect therapist. Let's not make matters worse. Your participation is at least as important as choosing the "best" therapist. But a good *match* is very important. Generally I would suggest you choose someone whom you feel comfortable with, but also someone who will challenge you when it's needed.

I find Irvin Yalom's thoughts here very insightful.[2] He noticed that people who are quieter, and might benefit from a less directive therapist, often pick someone who is too directive for them. A directive therapist might seem better at first if you are less comfortable speaking, but he or she may take too much responsibility for initiating the movement of the therapy. On the other hand, those clients who tend to talk a lot and need a more directive therapist to focus them tend to pick nondirective therapists. A therapist who isn't directive enough may let more spontaneous speakers ramble aimlessly.

The same issue of comfort versus challenge comes up in many ways: male or female, straight or gay, old or young, different culture or same culture. I would suggest that when in doubt, choose a therapist whom you feel more comfortable with, but discuss which issues you may need to be challenged on before you start.

Some characteristics of the therapist are an entirely personal choice: witty versus serious, formal versus informal, or natty dresser versus frumpy dresser. But the qualities of professionalism, dependability, and integrity are not optional. If there are any questions about how honest the therapist is (does her fee match what she advertised on her website?), about whether she will maintain appropriate boundaries (will she keep your confidentiality?), and about whether or not you can rely on her (did she return your call promptly; did she cancel your consultation twice?), discuss your concerns with the therapist to see how she responds, or move on to another therapist. If you don't feel comfortable with the therapist's responses, it does not bode well for your trust in her.

GOALS

Goal consensus leads to productive collaboration.[3] It will be important for you and your therapist to agree about what you want to achieve in therapy. Being clear on this at the outset is a good start. I'd suggest that you listen in the consultation to see if the prospective therapist has understood your concerns and goals. She might not sign on to your goals right away—that's not necessarily a bad thing; she's being honest, and perhaps very helpful if your goals are too low or too high. But eventually the two of you should be on the same page.

In general, setting goals can help us be effective in getting where we want to go. It makes sense to have a broad sense of what you want to accomplish when you start therapy. But setting the goals too specifically or concretely may limit you. Your goals may evolve as you become more aware of what's happening inside of you. An open mind may be the best mind to start therapy with.

Appendix B: *Are We There Yet?*
Stopping Therapy

"Are we there yet?"

How do you know when it's time to stop? The decision will be up to you, but your therapist should help you make the decision consciously. As I discussed in Chapter Four, there may be many reasons that you start to think about stopping—and you may not be aware of all of them. It may not be simply that you feel better and are ready to go. It could also be something less obvious—for instance, that you want to leave to avoid difficult issues, or that you don't feel like you deserve the benefits of therapy. These are only examples. Just consider that there may be more going on than meets the eye at this point.

Many clients say that they want to take a break when they really want to stop. This is a good time to exercise being direct with your therapist—and being honest with yourself. It's always best to process the decision with your therapist rather than to simply stop attending your sessions. The issue is not just *if* you stop therapy, it's also *how* you stop therapy. As I'll explain below, stopping therapy can be a really good thing—if it's done consciously.

HOW TO DECIDE

Here are some questions to ask yourself when considering stopping therapy:

- Have I met the goals that I originally came in with, and any other goals that I developed over time? (You may not reach them all, but at least be aware of anything left unfinished.)
- Is there anything I am trying to avoid by leaving?
- Do I have a good enough working relationship with myself (including the constructive unconscious) to continue the work on my own?
- Do I know and have a good working relationship with the different parts of my personality?
- Can I allow feelings to rise up inside of me, contain them, and use them as a source of direction?
- Have I achieved an appropriate level of responsibility?
- Do I have a clear and coherent sense of my life story?
- Can I use challenges as opportunities?

If you feel that you've run out of things to say or that you're not sure what to talk about, be present to what you're feeling in the moment during your session. If you feel basically good, review your goals for therapy and see whether you've met them and it's time to taper off. If you feel more flat, blank, or stuck it may mean that there is something you've been reluctant to talk about and it's blocking your progress.

IS THIS WORKING?

It may not be clear to you whether you're actually making progress. There may be times when you hit plateaus, or even feel like you're sliding downhill. There may be times when you leave sessions upset. None of these situations necessarily mean it's time to stop, but it does mean that it's time to talk about what's happening. Find out if your therapist feels that there is something you need to do differently to get things moving again. Let her know if you feel that she needs to do something differently.

Just because you revisit the same issue doesn't mean you're not progressing. Ideally those visitations add up to more awareness and eventual change—the visible change may just be more eventual than you'd like. And just because you've had a difficult week doesn't mean that the overall picture isn't better. I would suggest that you measure progress over many months—not over a single week.

But if you've already expressed your concerns about your progress with your therapist a number of times and it still feels stuck, then you may want to consult another therapist to get a second opinion, or to see if you can find a better fit.

Eventually it will be important to settle down with one therapist. If you change therapists too often, you won't get the full benefits of psychotherapy.

THE TERMINATION PHASE

Once you decide that you're ready to stop, take a few sessions to talk about the process. In order to get the most out of your work in therapy, don't end it with a phone message, email, or text. Go in and explore these themes with your therapist:

- What issues you've worked on,
- What progress you've accomplished,
- What worked well and what didn't work so well,
- What are the lessons that you want to take with you,
- What you'll continue working on on your own,
- How you'll continue with self-care afterward.

You should also talk about what it feels like to end the relationship. What, if any, memories and feelings does stopping therapy bring up? Does this remind you of any losses? Did anyone close to you suddenly die or leave? This period, known as the termination phase of treatment, can be helpful in healing previous wounds from separations that were not processed so consciously; the old, upsetting feelings can come to the surface in a much safer and more empathic environment, changing the feeling tone of the stored memory.

Some people slowly reduce the frequency of their sessions rather than stopping altogether. Others may choose to return occasionally for brush-up or booster sessions. Ideally you'll leave your therapist on good terms so that you can return for help if you hit a rough patch.

A conscious and well-planned termination period can not only be beneficial in a practical way, but also be a joyful time, leaving you with a sense of accomplishment and confidence. Then you can celebrate that all the work you've put in has been worth it.

Appendix C: *Does This Thing Work?* Research Evidence Supporting the Efficacy of Psychodynamic Psychotherapy

Many people considering psychotherapy want to know if there's any reason to believe that it will be effective. This is understandable: engaging in therapy requires a substantial investment of time, money, and energy. Thankfully, there is research that indicates that psychodynamic psychotherapy is effective for a wide variety of issues.

Research also indicates that it is more effective than other types of therapy for more complicated issues. To be clear, "more complicated" does not at all mean lower functioning. Many of the people that this refers to function quite well on the outside, but suffer a great deal on the inside. In fact it is often their "over-functioning" and all of the material rewards that come with that that make their situation more difficult to change.

I have included excerpts from three articles below. I've chosen these three because either they use large samples, or they review a large number of other studies. All of these reports were published in peer-reviewed journals, and each article references more studies if you'd like to do further research.

In a study published in 2008 in the *Journal of the American Medical Association*, "Effectiveness of Long-Term Psychodynamic Psychotherapy: A Meta-Analysis,"[1] researchers Falk Leichsenring and Sven Rabung conclude:

"In this meta-analysis, LTPP [long-term psychodynamic psychotherapy] was significantly superior to shorter-term methods of psychotherapy with regard to overall outcome, target problems, and personality functioning. Long-term psychodynamic psychotherapy yielded large and stable effect sizes in the treatment of patients with personality disorders, multiple mental disorders, and chronic mental disorders. The effect sizes for overall outcome increased significantly between end of therapy and follow-up."

In a 2011[2] follow-up study Leichsenring and Rabung updated their data and concluded that "LTPP is superior to less intensive forms of psychotherapy in complex mental disorders."

Jonathan Shedler, from the University of Colorado Denver School of Medicine, authored an article published in *American Psychologist*,[3] "The Efficacy of Psychodynamic Psychotherapy":

"Empirical evidence supports the efficacy of psychodynamic therapy. Effect sizes for psychodynamic therapy are as large as those reported for other therapies that have been actively promoted as 'empirically supported' and 'evidence based.' In addition, patients who receive psychodynamic therapy maintain therapeutic gains and appear to continue to improve after treatment ends. Finally, nonpsychodynamic therapies may be effective in part because the more skilled practitioners utilize techniques that have long been central to psychodynamic theory and practice. The perception that psychodynamic approaches lack empirical support does not accord with available scientific evidence and may reflect selective dissemination of research findings."

Consumer Reports published a study[4] that was reviewed in the journal *American Psychologist* by Martin Seligman,[5] an eminent psychotherapy researcher from the University of Pennsylvania. Here is Seligman's conclusion about the study:

"*Consumer Reports* published an article that concluded that patients benefited very substantially from psychotherapy, that long-term treatment did considerably better than short-term treatment, and that psychotherapy alone did not differ in effectiveness from medication plus psychotherapy. Furthermore, no specific modality of psychotherapy did better than any other for any disorder; psychologists, psychiatrists, and social workers did not differ in their effectiveness as treaters; and all did better than marriage counselors and long-term family doctoring. Patients whose length of therapy or choice of therapist was limited by insurance or managed care did worse."

He went on to say, "The *CR* study, then, is to be taken seriously—not only for its results and its credible source, but for its method."

No one can say for certain what results you'll get from psychotherapy. But with a therapist who's a good fit for you, and your earnest use of these tools, it's quite likely that therapy will help you to achieve a state of psychological well-being on which no price tag can be placed.

Acknowledgments

Much appreciation goes out to my many readers who helped shape this book, especially Kim White, Angela Bonavoglia , and Sylvia Perera, who all took time in the early stages of the book to provide helpful suggestions and assurance that the book was a good idea. April Castoldi, Jan Eisenman, Royce Froehlich, Wendy Jones, Kat Judd, Gigi Legendre, Beth Darlington, Eric Siegel, Arlin Roy, Richard Slade, and Kathryn Staley all helped with close readings, valuable feedback, and encouragement as the book was developing. Abigail Gehring gave superb editorial guidance and direction throughout the process. Thanks to Les Stein and Tony Lyons for quickly seeing the potential in the book.

To all my colleagues at the New York Association for Analytical Psychology and the C. G. Jung Institute of New York, and all my friends at the First Unitarian Society of Westchester: knowing that you were all behind me was priceless. Thanks to Aryeh Maidenbaum and Diana Rubin at the New York Center for Jungian Studies, and Janet Careswell at the C. G. Jung Foundation of New York for offering venues for me to develop my ideas. And much gratitude to my many teachers who helped shape me long before the book came to mind: Julie Bondanza, Soren Ekstrom, Don Ferrell, Harry Fogarty, Ron Grant, Don Kalsched, Maurice Krasnow, Dick Lewis, Alane Sauder MacGuire, Laurel Morris, Kathleen Ortiz, Robert Prince,

Mark Seides, Priscilla Rodgers, Sherry Salman, Susanne Short, Brian Sweeney, Warren Steinberg, and Joe Wagenseller.

And most of all, special thanks to Nancy, Zoe, and Thea for their love, patience, and constant support, and for teaching me what's most important.

About the Author

Gary Trosclair is a psychotherapist and psychoanalyst in private practice in New York City and Westchester County, New York. With twenty-five years' experience practicing and teaching in the field, he draws on a wide range of models to develop a comprehensive and flexible approach to human growth and healing. He has served as Director of Training at the C. G. Jung Institute of New York, where he continues to teach clinical courses. Through his blogging for Huffington Post and public speaking he bridges the gap between psychological theory and those who seek to use it to achieve change in their lives. To learn more about Dr. Trosclair visit his website at www.garytrosclair.com.

Endnotes

Introduction

1. Bohart, Arthur C. and Karen Tallman. 2010. "Clients: The Neglected Common Factor in Psychotherapy." In *The Heart and Soul of Change: Delivering What Works in Therapy*, edited by Barry L. Duncan, 83-111. Washington, DC: American Psychological Association.

    Nelson, R. A. and T. D. Borkovec. 1989. "Relationship of Client Participation to Psychotherapy." *J Behav Ther Exp Psychiatry* 20 (2):155-62.

    Orlinsky, D. E., M. Ronnestad, and U. Willutzki. 2004. "Fifty Years of Psychotherapy Process-Outcome Research: Continuity and Change." In *Bergin and Garfield's Handbook of Psychotherapy and Behavior Change* (5th Ed.), edited by M. J. Lambert, 307-90. New York: Wiley.

    Gomes-Schwartz, B. 1978. "Effective Ingredients in Psychotherapy: Prediction of Outcome from Process Variables." *J Consult Clin Psychol* 46 (5):1023-35.

    O'Malley, S. S., C. S. Suh, and H. H. Strupp. 1983. "The Vanderbilt Psychotherapy Process Scale: A Report on the Scale Development and a Process-Outcome Study." *J Consult Clin Psychol* 51 (4):581-6.

2. Kandel, Eric. 1998. (155) "A New Intellectual Framework for Psychiatry." *American Journal of Psychiatry*: 457-69.

3. Knekt, Paul, Olavi Lindfors, Maarit A. Laaksonen, Camilla Renlund, Peija Haaramo, Tommi Härkänen, and Esa Virtala. 2011. "Quasi-Experimental Study on the Effectiveness of Psychoanalysis, Long-Term and Short-Term Psychotherapy on Psychiatric Symptoms, Work Ability and Functional Capacity during a 5-Year Follow-Up." *Journal of Affective Disorders* 132 (1/2):37-47. doi: 10.1016/j.jad.2011.01.014.

Orlinsky, D. E., M. Ronnestad, and U. Willutzki. 2004. "Fifty Years of Psychotherapy Process-Outcome Research: Continuity and Change." In *Bergin and Garfield's Handbook of Psychotherapy and Behavior Change* (5th Ed.), edited by M. J. Lambert, 307-90. New York: Wiley.

Chapter One

1. Yalom, Irvin D. 1985. *The Theory and Practice of Group Psychotherapy*. New York: Basic Books. Pg. 75.

   Schwartz, Richard C. 1995. *Internal Family Systems Therapy*. New York: The Guilford Press.

2. Johnson, Robert. 1993. *Owning Your Shadow: Understanding the Dark Side of the Psyche*. San Fransisco: HarperCollins.

3. Winnicott, D. W. 1960. "Ego Distortion in Terms of True and False Self." In *The Maturational Processes and the Facilitating Environment*, 140-52. Madison, CT: International Universities Press.

4. Calvino, Italo. 1962. *The Nonexistent Knight & the Cloven Viscount; Two Short Novels*. New York: Random House.

5. Cozolino, Louis J. 2010. *The Neuroscience of Psychotherapy: Healing the Social Brain*. 2nd ed. New York: W. W. Norton & Co.

6. Gabbard, Glen O. 2000. "A Neurobiologically Informed Perspective on Psychotherapy." *The British Journal of Psychotherapy* 177 No. 2: 117-22.

Chapter Two

1. Nyklicek, Ivan, Lydia Temoshok, and Ad Vingerhoets. 2004. *Emotional Expression and Health*. New York: Brunner-Routledge.

2. Schore, Allan. 2012. *The Art of the Science of Psychotherapy*. New York: Norton.

3. Rottenberg, J., A. Cevaal, and A. J. Vingerhoets. 2008. "Do Mood Disorders Alter Crying? A Pilot Study." *Depression and Anxiety* 25(5): E9-15.

4. Beck, Aaron T. 1967. *Depression: Causes and Treatment*. Philadelphia: University of Pennsylvania Press.

5. Davenport, Donna S. 1991. "The Functions of Anger and Forgiveness: Guidelines for Psychotherapy with Victims." *Psychotherapy: Research, Practice, Training* Vol. 28(1): 140-44.

6. Gaylin, Willard. 2000. *Talk Is Not Enough: How Psychotherapy Really Works*. Boston: Little, Brown and Company.

7. Goleman, Daniel. 1994. *Emotional Intelligence*. New York: Bantam Books.

8. Damasio, Antonio R. 2005. *Descartes' Error: Emotion, Reason, and the Human Brain*. London: Penguin.

Chapter Three

1. Delsignore, A. and U. Schnyder. 2007. "Control Expectancies as Predictors of Psychotherapy Outcome: A Systematic Review." *Br J Clin Psychol* 46 (Pt 4):467-83. doi: 10.1348/014466507X226953.

Foon, A. E. 1987. "Review: Locus of Control as a Predictor of Outcome of Psychotherapy." *Br J Med Psychol* 60 (Pt 2):99-107.

2. Dave, Rachna, K. N. Tripathi, Poonam Singh, and Rakhi Udainiya. 2011. "Subjective Well-Being, Locus of Control, and General Self-Efficacy among University Students." *Amity Journal of Applied Psychology* 2 (1):28-32.

Judge, Timothy A., Amir Erez, Joyce E. Bono, and Carl J. Thoresen. 2002. "Are Measures of Self-esteem, Neuroticism, Locus of Control, and Generalized Self-Efficacy Indicators of a Common Core Construct?" *Journal of Personality and Social Psychology* 83(3): 693-710. doi: 10.1037/0022-3514.83.3.693.

Klonowicz, Tatiana. 2001. "Discontented People: Reactivity and Locus of Control as Determinants of Subjective Well-Being."

European Journal of Personality 15 (1):29-41. doi: 10.1002/per.387.

3. Lyubomirsky, S. 2001. "Why Are Some People Happier than Others? The Role of Cognitive and Motivational Processes in Well-Being." *Am Psychol* 56 (3):239-49.

4. Watters, Ethan. November 29, 2006. "DNA Is Not Destiny: The New Science of Epigenetics." *Discover.*

5. Cosmides, Leda and John Tooby. 1997. "Evolutionary Psychology: A Primer." http://www.cep.ucsb.edu/primer.html.

6. Gazzaniga, Michael S. 2011. *Who's in Charge? Free Will and the Science of the Brain.* 1st ed., Gifford Lectures. New York: HarperCollins.

7. Levine, Peter A. 1997. *Waking the Tiger: Healing Trauma, the Innate Capacity to Transform Overwhelming Experiences.* Berkeley, CA: North Atlantic Books.

8. van der Kolk, B. A. 1994. "The Body Keeps the Score: Memory and the Evolving Psychobiology of Post-Traumatic Stress." *Harv Rev Psychiatry* 1 (5):253-65.

9. Dijksterhuis, A. 2004. "Think Different: The Merits of Unconscious Thought in Preference Development and Decision Making." *Journal of Personality and Social Psychology* 87 (5):586-98.

10. Bargh, John A. 2011. "Unconscious Thought Theory and Its Discontents: A Critique of the Critiques." *Social Cognition* 29 (6):629-47.

Bargh, John A., Annette Lee-Chai, Kimberly Barndollar, Peter M. Gollwitzer, and Roman Trötschel. 2001. "The Automated Will: Nonconscious Activation and Pursuit of Behavioral Goals." *Journal of Personality and Social Psychology* 81 (6):1014-27.

Chapter Four

1. Norcross, John C. 2010. "The Therapeutic Relationship." In *The Heart and Soul of Change.* 113-42. Washington, DC: American Psychological Association.

Barber, J. P., M. B. Connolly, P. Crits-Christoph, L. Gladis, and L. Siqueland. 2000. "Alliance Predicts Patients' Outcome beyond In-Treatment Change in Symptoms." *Journal of Consulting and Clinical Psychology* 68:1027-32. doi: 10.1037/1949-2715.S.1.80.

2. Marziali, E., C. Marmar, and J. Krupnick. 1981. "Therapeutic Alliance Scales: Development and Relationship to Psychotherapy Outcome." *American Journal of Psychiatry* 138 (3):361-64.

3. Schore, A. N. 2009. "Relational Trauma and the Developing Right Brain: An Interface of Psychoanalytic Self-Psychology and Neuroscience." *Ann N Y Acad Sci* 1159:189-203. doi: 10.1111/j.1749-6632.2009.04474.x.

4. Levitt, Heidi, Mike Butler, and Travis Hill. 2006. "What Clients Find Helpful in Psychotherapy: Developing Principles for Facilitating Moment-to-Moment Change." *Journal of Counseling Psychology* 53 (3):314-24. doi: 10.1037/0022-0167.53.3.314.

5. Hill, C. E. and S. Knox. 2009. "Processing the Therapeutic Relationship." *Psychother Res* 19 (1):13-29. doi:10.1080/10503300802621206.

6. Siegel, Daniel. 2003. "An Interpersonal Neurobiology of Psychotherapy: The Developing Mind and the Resolution of Trauma." In *Healing Trauma: Attachment, Mind, Body, and Brain.* ed. Marion Solomon and Daniel Siegel. New York: W. W. Norton & Co.
Schore, A. N. 1996. "The Experience-Dependent Maturation of a Regulatory System in the Orbital Prefrontal Cortex and the Origin of Developmental Psychopathology." *Development and Psychopathology* 8:59-87.

7. Cozolino, Louis J. 2010. *The Neuroscience of Psychotherapy: Healing the Social Brain.* 2nd ed. New York: W. W. Norton & Co.

8. Spitz, R.A. 1945. "Hospitalism: An Inquiry into the Genesis of Psychiatric Conditions in Early Childhood." *Psychoanal Study Child* 1:53-74.

9. Schore, A. N. 1997. "Early Organization of the Nonlinear Right Brain and Development of a Predisposition to Psychiatric Disorders." *Development and Psychopathology* 9:595-631.

10. Santayana, George. 1905. *The Life of Reason: The Phases of Human Progress*. 5 vols. New York: C. Scribner's Sons.

11. Maroda, K. J. 1998. "Enactment: When the Patient's and the Analyst's Pasts Converge." *Psychoanalytic Psychology* 15:517-35.

12. Kabat-Zinn, Jon. 2013. *Full Catastrophe Living: Using the Wisdom of Your Body and Mind to Face Stress, Pain, and Illness*. Revised and updated edition. New York: Bantam Books.

Kohut, Heinz, Arnold Goldberg, and Paul E. Stepansky. 1984. *How Does Analysis Cure?* Chicago: University of Chicago Press.

Schore, Allan. 2012. *The Art of the Science of Psychotherapy*. New York: W. W. Norton & Co.

Chapter Five

1. Chödrön, Pema. 1997. *When Things Fall Apart: Heart Advice for Difficult Times*. Boston: Shambhala.

Chapter Six

1. Yalom, Irvin D. 1980. *Existential Psychotherapy*. New York: Basic Books.

2. International Society for the Study of Trauma and Dissociation. 2011. "Guidelines for Treating Dissociative Identity Disorder in Adults, Third Revision." *Journal of Trauma & Dissociation* 12 (2): 115-87. doi: http://dx.doi.org/10.1080/15299732.2011.537247.

"The DID [Dissociative Identity Disorder] patient should be seen as a whole adult person, with the identities sharing responsibility for daily life. Clinicians working with DID patients generally must hold the whole person (i.e., system of alternate identities) responsible for the behavior of any or all of the constituent identities, even in the presence of amnesia or the sense of lack of control or agency over behavior."

Chapter Seven

1. Byatt, A. S. 1998. *The Djinn in the Nightingale's Eye: Five Fairy Stories.* London: Knopf Doubleday.

2. Cozolino, op. cit. Pg. 306.

3. Cozolino, op. cit.

4. Through the use of a psychological assessment tool named the Adult Attachment Interview, psychologists have determined that those parents who have developed a more coherent story of their lives form better relationships with their children. The quality of their attachment can be predicted surprisingly well based on the quality of the coherence of the parent's life story.

   Behrens, K. Y., E. Hesse, and M. Main. 2007. "Mothers' Attachment Status as Determined by the Adult Attachment Interview Predicts Their 6-Year-Olds' Reunion Responses: A Study Conducted in Japan." *Dev Psychol* 43 (6):1553-67. doi: 10.1037/0012-1649.43.6.1553.

   Siegel, D. 1999. *The Developing Mind: How Relationships and the Brain Interact to Shape Who We Are.* New York: The Guilford Press.

5. Mehl-Madrona, Lewis. 2010. *Healing the Mind Through the Power of Story: The Promise of Narrative Psychology.* Rochester, VT: Bear & Company.

6. Bowlby, John. 1969. *Attachment.* New York: Basic Books.

7. Luborsky, Lester. 1984. *Principles of Psychoanalytic Psychotherapy: A Manual for Supportive-Expressive Treatment.* New York: Basic Books.

8. Stevens, Anthony. 2002. *Archetypes Revisited.* London: Taylor & Francis.

   Jung, C. G. 1959. *The Archetypes and the Collective Unconscious, Second Edition.* 20 vols. Vol. 9.1, *Bollingen Series XX.* New York: Princeton University Press.

9. Young, J. E., J. S. Klosko, and M. E. Weishaar. 2006. *Schema Therapy: A Practitioner's Guide.* New York: The Guilford Press.

10. Jung, C. G. 1934. "A Review of the Complex Theory." In *The Structure and Dynamics of the Psyche*, 92-104. Princeton: Princeton University Press.

Dieckmann, Hans. 1999. *Complexes: Diagnosis and Therapy in Analytical Psychology.* Wilmette, IL: Chiron Publications.

11. Nathanson, Donald L. 1992. *Shame and Pride: Affect, Sex, and the Birth of the Self.* 1st ed. New York: W. W. Norton & Co.

Siegel, P. and A. Demorest. 2010. "Affective Scripts: A Systematic Case Study of Change in Psychotherapy." *Psychother Res* 20 (4):369-87. doi: 10.1080/10503300903544240.

12. Karen, Robert. 1998. *Becoming Attached: First Relationships and How They Shape Our Capacity to Love.* Oxford: Oxford University Press.

Bowlby, John. 1969. *Attachment.* New York: Basic Books.

Chapter Eight

1. Cozolino, op. cit. Pg. 313.
2. Schacter, Daniel L., Joseph T. Coyle, and Harvard Center for the Study of Mind, Brain, and Behavior. 1995. *Memory Distortion: How Minds, Brains, and Societies Reconstruct the Past.* Cambridge, MA: Harvard University Press.
3. Kalsched, Donald. 1996. *The Inner World of Trauma: Archetypal Defenses of the Personal Spirit.* New York: Routledge.
4. Cozolino, op. cit. Pg. 311.

Chapter Nine

1. Ratey, John J. 2008. *Spark: The Revolutionary New Science of Exercise and the Brain.* Hachette Digital, Inc.
2. Weiss, M., J. W. Nordlie, and E. P. Siegel. 2005. "Mindfulness-Based Stress Reduction as an Adjunct to Outpatient Psychotherapy." *Psychother Psychosom* 74 (2):108-12. doi: 10.1159/000083169.
3. Kabat-Zinn, Jon. 2013. *Full Catastrophe Living: Using the Wisdom of Your Body and Mind to Face Stress, Pain, and Illness.* Revised and updated edition. New York: Bantam Books.

4. Wing, Rena R. and Robert W. Jeffery. 1999. "Benefits of Recruiting Participants with Friends and Increasing Social Support for Weight Loss and Maintenance." *Journal of Consulting and Clinical Psychology* 67 (1):132.

5. Tedeschi, Richard G. and Lawrence G. Calhoun. 2004. "Post-Traumatic Growth: Conceptual Foundations and Empirical Evidence." *Psychological Inquiry* 15 (1):1-18.
   Bonanno, G. A. 2004. "Loss, Trauma, and Human Resilience: Have We Underestimated the Human Capacity to Thrive after Extremely Aversive Events?" *Am Psychol* 59 (1):20-8. doi: 10.1037/0003-066X.59.1.20.

6. Gilbert, Daniel. 2006. *Stumbling on Happiness.* 1st ed. New York: A. A. Knopf.

7. Johnson, Robert A. 1986. *Inner Work: Using Dreams and Active Imagination for Personal Growth.* 1st ed. San Francisco: Harper & Row.
   Stuckey, Heather and J. Nobel. 2010. "The Connection Between Art, Healing, and Public Health: A Review of Current Literature." *American Journal of Public Health* 100 (2):254.

8. Kerner, E. A. and M. R. Fitzpatrick. 2007. "Integrating Writing into Psychotherapy Practice: A Matrix of Change Processes and Structural Dimensions." *Psychotherapy (Chicago)* 44 (3):333-46. doi: 10.1037/0033-3204.44.3.333.

9. Pennebaker, James W. and Janel D. Seagal. 1999. "Forming a Story: The Health Benefits of Narrative." *Journal of Clinical Psychology* 55 (10):1243-54.

10. White, Michael and Epston, David. 1990. *Narrative Means to Therapeutic Ends.* New York: W. W. Norton & Co.

11. Baikie, Karen A. and Kay Wilhelm. 2005. "Emotional and Physical Health Benefits of Expressive Writing." *Advances in Psychiatric Treatment* September (11):338-46. doi:10.1192/apt.11.5.338.

12. Bolton, Gillie. 1999. *The Therapeutic Potential of Creative Writing: Writing Myself.* Philadelphia: Jessica Kingsley.

13. Slattery, Dennis Patrick. 2012. *Riting Myth, Mythic Writing: Plotting Your Personal Story.* 1st ed. Carmel, CA: Fisher King Press.

14. Malchiodi, Cathy A. 2007. *The Art Therapy Sourcebook.* New York: McGraw-Hill.

15. Stevens, Anthony. 1995. *Private Myths: Dreams and Dreaming.* Cambridge, MA: Harvard University Press.

16. Whitmont, Edward C. and Sylvia Brinton Perera. 1991. *Dreams, a Portal to the Source.* London: Routledge.

17. Johnson, Robert A. 1986. *Inner Work: Using Dreams and Active Imagination for Personal Growth.* 1st ed. San Francisco: Harper & Row.

18. Fosshage, James L. and Clemens A. Loew. 1978. *Dream Interpretation: A Comparative Study.* New York: SP Medical & Scientific Books.

19. Gino, Francesca and Michael Norton. August 23, 2013. "Why Rituals Work." *Scientific American.*

Chapter Ten

1. Seery, M. D., R. J. Leo, S. P. Lupien, C. L. Kondrak, and J. L. Almonte. 2013. "An Upside to Adversity?: Moderate Cumulative Lifetime Adversity Is Associated with Resilient Responses in the Face of Controlled Stressors." *Psychol Sci* 24 (7):1181–89. doi: 10.1177/0956797612469210.

2. Cozolino, op. cit. Pg. 20.

3. Campbell, Joseph. 1949. *The Hero with a Thousand Faces.* Princeton: Princeton University Press.

4. Tedeschi, Richard G. and Lawrence G. Calhoun. 2004. "Post-Traumatic Growth: Conceptual Foundations and Empirical Evidence." *Psychological Inquiry* 15 (1):1–18.

5. Schaefer, J. and R. Moos. 1992. "Life Crises and Personal Growth." In *Personal Coping: Theory, Research, and Application,* edited by B. Carpenter, 149–70. Westport, CT: Praeger.

6. Tedeschi, op. cit.

7. Tedeschi, op. cit.

Park, C. L., L. H. Cohen, and R. L. Murch. 1996. "Assessment and Prediction of Stress-Related Growth." *J Pers* 64 (1):71–105.

8. Tedeschi, op. cit.

9. Bowman, Marilyn. 1997. *Individual Differences in Post-Traumatic Response: Problems with the Adversity-Distress Connection.* Mahwah, NJ: Lawrence Erlbaum Associates.

10. Park, C. L., op. cit.

11. Taylor, Jill Bolte. 2008. *My Stroke of Insight: A Brain Scientist's Personal Journey.* 1st Viking ed. New York: Viking.

12. Ratey, op. cit.

Afterword

1. Barth, J., T. Munder, H. Gerger, E. Nuesch, S. Trelle, H. Znoj, P. Juni, and P. Cuijpers. 2013. "Comparative Efficacy of Seven Psychotherapeutic Interventions for Patients with Depression: A Network Meta-Analysis." *PLoS Med* 10 (5):e1001454. doi: 10.1371/journal.pmed.1001454.

2. Yalom, op. cit.

3. Norcross, John C. 2010. "The Therapeutic Relationship." In *The Heart and Soul of Change,* 113–42. Washington, DC: American Psychological Association.

Appendix C

1. Leichsenring, F. and S. Rabung. 2008. "Effectiveness of Long-Term Psychodynamic Psychotherapy: A Meta-Analysis." *JAMA* 300 (13):1551–65. doi: 10.1001/jama.300.13.1551.

2. Leichsenring, F. and S. Rabung. 2011. "Long-Term Psychodynamic Psychotherapy in Complex Mental Disorders: Update of a Meta-Analysis." *Br J Psychiatry* 199 (1):15–22. doi: 10.1192/bjp. bp.110.082776.

3. Shedler, J. 2010. "The Efficacy of Psychodynamic Psychotherapy." *Am Psychol* 65 (2):98–109. doi: 10.1037/a0018378.

4. *Consumer Reports*. November 1995. "Mental Health: Does Therapy Help?" 734-39.

5. Seligman, M. E. 1995. "The Effectiveness of Psychotherapy: The *Consumer Reports* Study." *American Psychologist* 50 (12):965-74.

Index